CAMPUS to CORPORATE

A concise street smart guide to world class career success!

NAVEEN CHANDRA

Copyright © 2017 Naveen Chandra

All rights reserved.

ALL RIGHTS RESERVED. No part of this book may be reproduced or transmitted in any form whatsoever, electronic, or mechanical, including photocopying, recording or by any informational storage or retrieval system without the expressed written, dated and signed permission from the author.

Author: Naveen Chandra R
Title: Campus to Corporate
ISBN-13: 9781973172550
Category: Business & Economics/Careers
www.naveenchandra.in

LIMITS OF LIABILITY / DISCLAIMER OF WARRANTY:

The author and publisher of this book have used their best efforts in preparing this material. The author and publisher make no representation or warranties with respect to the accuracy, applicability or completeness of the contents. They disclaim any warranties (expressed or implied), or merchantability for any particular purpose. The author and publisher shall in no event be held liable for any loss or other damages, including but not limited to special, incidental, consequential, or other damages. The information presented in this publication is compiled from sources believed to be accurate, however the publisher assumes no responsibility for errors or omissions. The information in this publication is not intended to replace or substitute professional advice. The author and publisher specifically disclaim any liability, loss or risk that is incurred as a consequence, directly or indirectly, of the use and application of any of the contents of this work.

Published by:
M/s Yukta Enterprises,
Mysore – Karnataka, India.

DEDICATION

To the reader; who aspires to craft life by design.

CONTENTS

Acknowledgments	9
Preface	11
Introduction	13
PART I – THE BEGINNING	17

1 **The Dilemma** 21

- Power of Choice
- Options
- Campus Recruitment
- Life after Campus
- Interviews
- Evening or Weekend education
- A Personal life stage
- Action Exercise

PART II – JUNIOR MANAGEMENT	37

2 **The Alignment** 41

- Fresher days
- A Question
- Reality
- Work with a Senior
- Team Player
- Street Smart
- Financial Education
- IT – A Service provider Industry
- Understand Organization
- Enterprise Resources planning

3 **Learn As Much** 55

- Begin with end mind
- Abroad Career
- MBA Time
- Changing Jobs
- Certifications
- Toast masters
- Entrepreneur Mindset
- Designations
- Appraisal Process
- A Personal Life stage
- Action Exercise

PART III – MIDDLE MANAGEMENT 71

4 **Cross Skilling** 75

- Management
- Verticals & Horizontals
- Functional Learning
- Process Orientation
- Marketing, Sales and Presales
- Professional Etiquettes
- Basic Management Lessons
- Industry Overview

5 **Managing Self** 83

- Self Help
- Clarity
- A Passion Test
- Values
- Wheel of Life
- Vision
- Goals
- Smart Goals
- Assessments
- Crisis in Job
- The Inner Circle
- Thank you for Firing me

6 **Leading Teams** 99

- Team Spirit
- Team Work
- Best Practices
- Effectiveness at Work
- Right G & O
- Gen Y
- Management Vs Leadership
- Evidences of a Good Team

7 **Financial Freedom** 109

- Why Freedom
- Start Early
- Our Excuses
- 360 Degree Financial Planning
- A Good Debt
- Business of Investing
- Rich Vs not so rich
- Arrive at right corpus
- Freedom Formulae
- A Personal Life stage
- Action Exercise

PART IV – SENIOR MANAGEMNT 125

8 **The Big Picture** 129

- Think BIG
- A shared Vision
- Merger, Acquisition and Joint Venture
- Fund Raising
- Angel Investor and Venture Capital
- Initial Public Offer
- Top & Bottom lines
- Turning as Investor
- A Social Enterprise

9 **Living the Legacy** 139

- A Legend
- Making of a Leader
- Living the Legacy
- Run your own race
- Who am I
- What should I do
- No excuse at death
- Leaders Grow Leaders
- The 21st Century Leadership
- A Personal Life stage
- Action Exercise

Meet the Author 153

ACKNOWLEDGMENT

I thank my mentors for refining my thoughts;
I bow down with reverence for those moments of truth.
They are priceless.

PREFACE

Career growth in IT industry can be nonlinear. People with hard work and talent can make to top very fast. There are efforts to define the path for career growth by organizations. True journey is transforming from an employee mindset to an entrepreneur mindset and then to that of a leader mindset. This is what it's really about. I chalked out my path as most of us do; by trial and error and then choose what works. I went a little ahead to choose what inspires. It made enormous differences in all spheres of my life.

While I was leading cross culture IT teams, I have noted down the best practices I came across with multiple customers including some of fortune 500 companies. Through my corporate training I had people from all career levels sharing their concerns and looking for right direction. It wasn't very different. I found same issues were raised over and again from different corners. People who joined from colleges of repute, those who studied abroad, interns from different countries, multinational colleagues and sometimes from senior positions who had been successful in earning lots of money.

I found people were so busy in running and even overwhelmed by it. Driven by management towards business results, I observed men and women slowly lose the charm of inspired living, resulting in dragging themselves to the office. A few retained the clarity of what they wanted in life amidst the pressure of work and family by achieving magical work life balance. I observed 90:10 rule applies here.

People had begun with lofty intentions yet get carried away taking easier options while life offers choices. Over a period of time they reach to a point in thinking that this is what life is all about; totally forgetting that their choices had led to where they are now.

Killing dreams living mediocre.

If we know a path beforehand, our choices would vastly differ and so would be the results. Saves of our precious time which can then be employed for a better cause.

So an attempt is made thinking of a person who is stepping on to a corporate ladder. Here, I collated items I learnt through my experience. I had repeatedly tested these ideas with different teams and religiously taught to the teams I led. I found they produce similar results whosoever practices them. I organized these in a relevant manner to comprehend and put them into practice easily.

I acknowledge every support and guidance received in doing so. The books and websites I referred are listed at the end of each of the four parts. Readers may go through them for enhancing knowledge further.

INTRODUCTION

You have passed out of campus....*SO WHAT?*

Or say... *what next* ...to be on a milder tone. Milder because you are yet to get used to the tone of employer who writes your monthly pay cheque !

Most of us as students for years did not take up time and effort to figure out what our passion is about; which is supposed to wake us up with zeal every morning to make difference in our life.

Longer we wait for the things to happen, more we try beat around the bush. Our mind comes up with excuses and success in real world moves apart. We have been with the flow of life, we did what we have been taught to do and we did not to use our creative mind to become street smart.

Result is first hand now; confusion, lack of self-confidence and frustration. Easier to call it quarter life crisis. Sometime this state may take few more years to show up with more or less similar feelings, we then call it mid-life crisis. Worst of it may come as frustration at death bed, with a feeling of not put our best with the talents and time we had, at our disposal.

We can ignore our inner calling and continue with the flow. Calling may come back a few more times in life. And haunt us severely, till such time we sit with ourselves and do a deeper introspection. A nature's way of reminding that you are not ordinary.

We can also avoid all together such efforts and remain mediocre for rest of our life, blaming everyone around us for the situation we are in. Calling will stop.

It's time now to try different things. Good point is before such situation becomes evident in our life, pages that follow, have some solutions to make course correction.

In subsequent pages we learn to take a sincere stock of things, from where we are now, then understand, define and arrive at the clarity required for us in pursuit of our dreams.

I am yet to find a successful person who is not passionate about what he or she is doing.

The step we are able to see now, we will take that with faith and it will lead to other invisible steps of the ladder. Once the *Big Picture* thinking becomes natural, we will know whether our ladder is leaned on right wall or not.

We will find out our passion and purpose. Practice right usage of our time and knowledge toward the primary aim of achieving souls content. Honest approach begins with questioning every answer our mind gives and figuring out is it an excuse or a reason. First lesson; here after we will ask five times *why* for every answer our mind gives.

Book focuses predominantly on Indian IT service provider industry. Nevertheless I think these ideas should be applicable to other industry segments also.

Book is organized as following four convenient parts.

- Part 1 – The Beginning – Focuses on a campus pass out with or without job.

- Part 2 - Junior Management - First 5 years - What should be done in early years at work.

- Part 3 - Middle Management - Next 10 years - Transforming oneself and preparation required for next level.

- Part 4 - Senior Management - Last 10 years or more – Sharing the knowledge and living a legacy.

Reader can begin with most relevant part, chapter or topic applicable to their situation and then go to the next topic or simply follow chronological. Every part has focus area, personal life stage and action exercises.

All learning need not fall in the same order as given in the contents. Readers can focus learning the related points as and when it makes sense along with topic of interest, allowing street smart way of getting ahead.

Let's simplify as we go further with CAMPUS to CORPORATE.

You now have a gold mine of proven strategies for making it right first time.

All the best!

Live by heart!

Naveen Chandra R
October, 2017
Bangalore, India.

NAVEEN CHANDRA

PART I

THE BEGINNING

FOCUS AREA

This section is designed considering the state of mind of students, who may need a sense of direction towards their career.

Focus is on the situation of having you passed out of the Campus with a technical or management education. We will take commonsense approach to look at the power of choice based on the options at hand. Then learn to become committed in turning our dreams into a reality. While staying inspired throughout the journey in order to achieve it.

We can refer to 80/20 rule here. 20 percent of students have the necessary clarity and have enrolled to next level of action with confidence. While 80 percent needs a direction to be part of those 20 percent in future.

When people are not equipped with proper guidance, they get biased with the opinions of majority. Repeated delay or failure in endeavors can put most into a lower confidence level. This may lead to trying out different paths simultaneously having below average or no results. While one is not focused energy dissipates in multiple directions.

To stay afloat with positivity, keeping target always on top of mind is a minimum requirement.

Action exercises are listed at the end of this part. Following those would help to keep up the spirit consistently. Once students have necessary ideas and understanding on what to experience in the career, their progress can skyrocket.

Let's go through these ideas.

| 1 |

THE DILEMMA

Beginning of all things are small – Cicero.

Power of Choice

Life is made up of series of choices.

Making no choice in a given situation also proves it to be a choice!. Right choice comes with awareness. Better the awareness better would be our choices. I observed there is no justification needed when we do a right thing. A right choice which is based on our values can give us long term results.

People come with different background and experiences. Expecting always a right circumstance, can be a trap. What is important is get to the right perspective, irrespective of the wrongs which are within us and around us. We might have no control on the consequences. However it is important to understand, the choices we make today do have some degree of control on them.

When we choose comfort over conflict, rest over struggle, ease versus glory we are defining our future. We have two primary choices here. First one, be willing to confront and learn the lessons. Second, change our attitude towards the problem; otherwise it will continue to haunt us for life time. Life is short to risk it.

Same thinking, same activities over years would not give us very different results. The future we can see now, is the future we are going to get. One may look back at his or her past to confirm this. All our choices has resulted in the situation we are in now. Being conscious of what is being sowed now, is the first choice every one of us can make.

Yes, chances would favor; luck strikes but not always.

Being aware of what we seek to experience in life, what skills are needed for such experience and what kind of attitude we need to develop, matters most. It applies to work, life and ourselves. It is necessary to have a constant watch on ourselves, where we are heading towards and what are we becoming in that process.

Energy and passion stem automatically when we start with the conviction that we are the designers of our life and nothing happens to us by itself except deteriorate. Once our route to the glory becomes clearer, we realize we have the biggest asset with us. That is our self.

Let's tap that power of choice to make us better each day. It can spare us from bitter feeling of having not lived the life fully when it all gets over.

Options

While you are out of campus and you have following options to consider for your future.

- You have completed graduation, post-graduation, have couple of job offers on hand and not able to decide where to join
- You are looking at higher studies be technical or management related, at prestigious colleges around the world
- You are looking at competitive or public services exams to serve at banking, government or military services
- Continue to do family business
- Getting into a teaching profession
- Study abroad and pursue career there till retirement
- Just want to start where you get option to do so
- You don't know what to do
- You may try copy what others are doing
- You have no guide to reach out who can talk to you at your level of maturity and give the clarity which you need
- Parents did not do that as they were busy with their career
- You may think your parent's ideas are outdated and their approach does not inspire you anymore
- You are looking at role models on media, think and dream about it, but don't know where to begin

- You are degrading slowly in your mind, doing whatever you were asked to do

- You did not wait for others opinion, you started freelancing based on what you learnt in education

- You are clear what is that satisfies you and inspires

- You don't have *money* thinking because throughout your life you had no scarcity of it, somebody provided them

- You are thinking *money* defines everything because you lacked that resource in your life so far.

Whatever may be your thoughts are, you are rightly positioned where you are now in your life's journey. Having a *big picture* where it all leads to before beginning of the journey can make enormous difference, compared to those who don't have.

Once we have 360 degree view of our life and career in particular, our ability to do better happens at day one. We will live more in now than in yesterday nor in tomorrow, a starting point for being successful.

Begin with picking up those industries or work areas which excites you. where you wish to make your career. Then identify those companies you wish to work for. It may be little difficult for a beginner, but same principle can be used in future years too.

We are going to do that by studying the pages that follow. Mere reading will not help. When we study, we make notes of those points which are important for us and list the actionable. This leads to more effectiveness at learning.

Campus Recruitment

This is an easier place to begin the career, helps to put yourself on a fast track. Different companies come to college door step and talk about their organization history, mission, vison and values. Companies may a quick overview and the general career path for a beginner.

It would be nice to hear from many companies. It can lead to confusion on which one to choose to join, because everything looks fancy and colorful on PPTs. Beginners will have difficulty to understand the numbers, ability to grasp the market capitalization, geography and nature of services.

Here are quick tips which one to focus to help oneself.

- Talk to your college senior who is working in that company, to understand their work culture and work ethics

- Understand clearly what are you looking for – a job, Career or Money

- Know that you would need a few years to experience the entire gamut of functional areas, to understand an organization functions. We are simplifying them in pages ahead.

- If you have a choice to peruse a job immediately, then do that on priority, as compared to higher studies, family business or self-employment.

- A job exposes you to be realistic. Human interactions and their expectations can only be learnt on-hands. This experience will aid whatever area you wish to continue later, be it higher studies or entrepreneurship

- Dreams are good, when they are based on the reality, they become better

- Reality of work life is not fully available at the campus. Though a few universities do look at such possibilities through interns and by providing job preparation trainings at the campus

- Attending talks from industry people helps to bridge that gap, take such sessions on priority

- Practice business case study debates - It may be part of your curriculum or pick them from Harvard business review articles. Come up with your points, share them in group, practicing more cases will help more

- Learn to articulate your points in a manner which invoke curiosity in others to listen. It aids to a great extent on how well one can express, listen to others and appreciate the diversity of views the group presents

- Here technology and core competencies required are assumed to be met. Because you are already qualified for the campus-interview based on the cut off percentages or other norms as set in your academy

- Learn to know what you want to do in life and how would you perceive yourself over 3, 5, 10 or more years from now

- Leadership is about taking ownership for what we do and what we don't. It starts with oneself

- By understanding everything is up to us, we are gearing up for an opportunity to create a future we are going to be proud of

Most of the beginners at this stage are following what others are doing. Their parents are biased with what others children are doing and insist on doing the same for their children.

When we don't take up the efforts for getting into details and analyzing what we really want out of our employment and in our life, we are heading to mediocrity.

Nothing happens by itself except deterioration.

In the pages that follow we will learn how to identify our true self. Identify those areas which we are passionate about, so that we don't need to work a single day in life. Because we are so excited doing what we want to do in life, then there is no stress.

Life after Campus

It is a fact that most may not get recruited via campus selection. Remaining students may need to choose different ways based on their socio- economic background.

Easier profession for anyone out there is to teach to a lower semester or grades. People who have interest in teaching profession can do well at it by having a master degree or specialization.

Alternatively people can undergo specialized trainings which offers a guaranteed job placement or interviews with other companies. They are more in demand. These technologies vary from time to time and as per market conditions.

Working for learning and not for earning is a right approach, if one can take it that way. If you focus only on getting a job and getting paid for it, then chances are that your mind gets satisfied with it. If you have lofty ideas then constant thinking is essential to keep oneself moving forward right way.

Learn how to do fishing and not just focus on getting a fish for food each day. Once that difference is known, one can find own ways which can inspire him or her for life time. Till that happens, staying positive is essential and true positivity takes time and effort.

Here are a few tips which can help in that direction.

- On and Off - Inspiration is possible to anyone. Watch a movie of a favorite hero and feel the energy for few hours to few days

- Listen to an inspiring talk or watch TED videos, or even read inspirational books. But nothing lasts forever. Jim rohn, puts it well, *'Motivation is like bathing, both are required daily.'* Consistency in efforts can produce lasting results

- There is a saying a one can have inspiration for 30 minutes, 30 days or 3 months. A person who is inspired for 3 years to 30 years can make a difference in the world. That is what everyone of us should aim for

- First get a clarity on the career front, on what is possible and what is not. You can become anything but not everything

- Listen to your heroes often in whatever ways, they work

- Read often from those chosen authors to whom you have respect.

- Attend seminars or workshops happening around. Events in bookmyshow.com can give some hints

- Associate with people who are better than you

- People who knew early in life what they wish to become and work towards it usually achieve what they aim at

- Majority are not even aware what they really want from career. Mostly their thinking depends on the people nearer to them. Success cannot be achieved this way

- One can always do a thing in two ways, either enjoying it or doing it reluctantly. Results achieved would differ vastly.

Interviews

Take as much job interviews as possible. Do that till you feel comfortable in attending it, irrespective of the results associated. Each attempt helps you become better. Attending an interview requires preparation for getting into a proper mental framework.

Here are a few tips which can be handy.

- Dress professionally. Have a genuine smile on face. People can make out a lot about you in just first look and opinions are set subconsciously. Rest of the interactions generally will be to match what is already made up in the mind of the interviewer.

- As we progress in career, developing an unbiased and free mind open enough to see things objectively has to developed. It can begin by looking at the good part of an event in every situation. It will prove to be a greater asset to oneself.

- Start practicing a few lines on *who you are* and *what makes you interesting* from the point of view of the interviewer. Make it very effective one, do rehearsals. Most of the questions which follows are usually an extension of what you already told about yourself. Technically called as two minute elevator pitch.

- Practice your elevator pitch often till you master it. While you are preparing for an interview, develop understanding on the holistic picture of the industry you are trying to make mark at.

- Get to know the global players name, the local competitors and the top ten in the industry. Both at organization level and as individuals, who have made remarkable contribution in that arena. This gives you an ability to speak easily about what you want do in that segment starting from where you are today and to what you want to be in future. Remember future is created every day.

- Rich Dad says it is top 10% of any industry who actually makes fortune. 90:10 rule. Knowing industry helps to take interviews confidently. It can help even in the stock market investments by knowing how that industry will thrive in future.

- Develop habit of holistic or big picture thinking. When we have complete overview understanding the minor aspects of it become easier and possible. Start there.

- Typical question – Tell me more about you?. Interviewer will ask this by looking at your resume. Following questions can be expected during the conversation.

  Why do you think we need to hire you?
  What do you see yourself as in next 3 – 5 years?
  Tell us more about your strengths and weaknesses?

- Interestingly, you will be asked almost same questions at different levels of your career. Every encounter with senior business leader in the corporate world can be used for your advantage. Provided you know how to project yourself as positive, goal oriented and ready to learn kind of individual; this is what employers look for.

- Interviews do not get over once you get a job. They are continuous part of career life. Considering the IT services segment, when one customer project gets over you would be interviewed again for a new project by a different customer.

- Free time between the projects is often termed as *Bench*. Time here typically used for enhancing skills and competencies.

- Develop an attitude that, each interview you attend builds you and prepares for better opportunities in future. That way any disappointment that might follow after the interviews can be minimized or even eliminated.

- Stay updated with the industry news.

- Being honest on what you know and ability to tell that in a manner which can be appreciated by your interviewer is the skill one should develop.

- Record your performance in audio or video formats wherever possible. It can hint where you have fared well. It gives an opportunity to review objectively and accept your inadequacies.

- Selection can be based on the need being met, skill wise. Also on the Interviewer perception about you that you have the necessary fundamentals which can be fine-tuned with trainings or on hand jobs.

- It's never about pleasing the interviewer. It's about being yourself, showcasing yourself as what you are and projecting a proactive learner image.

- Take guidance on how to write in a resume. Unnecessary information makes interviewer lose focus and may even discard the case. Be precise on what you are looking for. If you are open for any kind of role which matches to your skillsets you can mention that too. Always highlight your significant achievements.

- Be prepared for lifelong learning, in fact true learning starts after your academics are over and life learnings never end.

I have observed at higher level job interviews, people look for compatibility as an individual who can fit rightly into the existing team culture. They look for a person who can enhance the collective efforts positively. Here comes the importance of individual attitude, a very fundamental nature of us. It has taken years to form, by way of upbringing, life experiences and adopted beliefs. This is not easily modifiable. However the skills as required to perform at the job can always be learned.

Evening or Weekend Education

IT Industry has some options where people can pursue weekend engineering studies while working at the office premises during week days. Generally teaching sessions are held at the class rooms of colleges which are tied up with corporates.

Similarly campus recruits may have employer trainings conducted at their college premises towards the preparation for the job roles.

Weekend education is a good option while it take care of immediate income need and as well enhance individual professional competency over time.

However these options are good in the initial stages of the career where one have relatively less responsibility of deliverables. Most of the qualification aids to get an interview from the employers. Whereas progress in the career are usually based on the results one produce.

A PERSONAL LIFE STAGE

This section touches your personal life while you are working on your career life. At this juncture, you would be having ample time for yourself to identify your interests. Lesser responsibilities as a single person aids enough time to pursue your interest whole heartedly.

Utilize this time to read the biographies of people you respect and want learn from their example. Whoever may be your role model or hero; try understand why they are your role model and then try to develop those qualities in yourself.

Role model can give us direction for our thinking and to get inspired how they achieved their distinction. It can be a person next door, family member or a relative or even a public figure.

Arrive at what are the areas which you wish to focus and then spend time in learning at those areas. It can pay you a huge dividend. Don't do anything because you don't know what else to do. If somebody is doing something just don't copy, it may work for them and may not be for others. All your interests are going to make sense to you over a period of time, it can make a dot in the circle of your life.

Ensure you have limited number of interest so that something concrete can be achieved in that area. At a higher level one may need to choose between 1 or 2, giving up the good for best.

Spending time for entertainment should be a way of learning in that area. Change of work is rest as told by Arthur Canon. Soon one realize this aspect, one can get maximum out of his or her life.

ACTION EXERCISE

A Typical Day

- Get up before sunrise. Do 30 minutes exercise and 30 minutes meditation. It helps more than any other things.

- Close a day by 22:00. Dinner preferably before 19.30.

- Segment your day for work, food and rest.

- Staying physically fit and being mentally alert is first step to achieve more in 24 hours that everybody has.

Learning Areas

- Networks with people. Stay in the group of positive people.

- Check out employment bureaus, HR consultants & Training with placement opportunities.

- Start small, with where you are and what you have.

- Consider to learn an additional language which can help to connect with more people on business.

- Identify your interest areas. Taking action in the direction of your goals. It relieves the worry and stress of not getting things done.

Recommendations

- Social media can be a trap; choose cautiously on the time you spend there.

- Connecting on social media towards the focus areas, interests and for business networking can help immensely.

- Read Dale Carnegie books -

- How to stop worrying and start living

- How to win friends and influence people.

PART II

JUNIOR MANAGEMENT

NAVEEN CHANDRA

FOCUS AREA

You are now recruited for a job in a corporate. You are part of junior management with age group between 20 – 30 years.

This stage of life is interesting, since you are now leading an independent life, with lots of hope, enthusiasm and vigor. New things, new places, new foods and new people will be of interest. Any entertainment which is adding value on learnings or on hobbies can be pursued immensely.

If you are one of those who don't know 'what else to do', entertainment or passing of time with what others usually do, then exercise caution immediately to avoid falling into that bracket.

While on job, you tend to pick up your own way of comparing with peers. Their designation, income and percentage of increment received, vehicle they own etc. While comparing can breed a healthy competition, it seldom happens if we are not cautious enough. If you really want to compare, then do it on the net worth of the individual. Also on the potential he or she is displaying now which can accelerate their growth in future.

This helps immensely to turn your focus inwards. All outside successes are result of inside successes. If you don't learn to take things objectively you resent others progress and bitterness which comes out of it spoils your positivity more than anything else.

Best way to understand the compensation package is that, it will be equaling to the value you add to your organization. Practicality may differ. However on an average this formulae works well and help to reassert on what worth of value we are adding each day to our organization.

Let's focus now on how to get best out of your junior management period.

NAVEEN CHANDRA

|2|

ALIGNMENT

Well begun is half done – Aristotle

Fresher Days

She waved her hand to a few colleagues who have recently joined from same college through campus recruitment.

All of them were attired in new clothes were rejoicing and had success looks and some even tried business wares of white and black combination. Whole world was a good place to be at, as their struggles had paid off. Almost each celebrated their success in their own ways for couple of days stretching to couple of months.

Nothing wrong, you deserve.

Roughly, after 6 - 8 months, their faces were dull, they looked weathered and exhausted. They still had a dream job and a great career ahead.

They were exhausted with travel to office which takes almost 2- 3 hours a day, like in most of the metros of India. They were being trained with multiple skills required to work and waiting for a project.

In technical words they were on *bench*, waiting for work while developing themselves fit for different work areas and multiple programing languages.

They started comparing themselves with people who were on project assignments. Believing that those with projects have better chance to learn with the accelerated speed and thus their progress in career can be faster.

Anticipating an infinite amount of time on *bench*, most are turning negative themselves in a seemingly positive environment of garden, fountains and food courts. Comparison has begun even before the career taking its right shape. You will know how this factor alone contributes much of the job dissatisfaction in the coming years if you are not alert.

People who are dissatisfied will start discussing those things. Negativity broods company. Repeatedly hearing those discussions can bring down the spirit of positivity about future.

It may also be noted, few aspirants continue to stay on *bench*, expecting a better project assignment and giving up the projects which may be at their discretion to join. While waiting has both pros and cons, depends on how well you utilized that period.

Usually real learning begins on the job. However well we were trained on a subject practicality always matters. Hence starting early hands on job works good in long run.

A Question

Why are you working ?, Ask this question daily, until you get an answer. An answer, which you cannot deny however well one may like to sugarcoat.

I don't need your answer. You need to know your answer. Because next 20 years each day 8 hours at office is going to take major a portion of your life. In fact the essence of your life itself will be spent out there. Hence it would be wise to arrive at an answer and be clear at it.

It may take a few weeks to few months or few years to arrive at a right answer. I also found the answer which comes immediately the moment you hear the question first time, is generally the right one. Whatever answer mind gives, keep asking why so. Continue this until the one day you know that you have a right answer.

It will be for a job, career or money.

When you say it is for a job sake; it means your interests are elsewhere but you need the money a job may offer, or the respect for being employed that you can get in community, excitement of working for big brands etc. come here.

While the answer is for career; it means you have a long term view of seeing yourself in the CXO level of the company you work for. You clearly know this one aim satisfies you most .

Money, is an answer of entrepreneur. They are working to learn and understand how business works. They would learn here the way of doing business, dealing with different levels of people, be it team mates, management, customers and vendors. They also learns about how facilities team functions, those who help individuals with services of food, transport, stationary, security etc. Then go out try himself or herself on the ideas they values most.

Whatever may be your answer, that can change over period of time. To progress authentically you need to arrive at an answer. It looks tough to do this exercise, but result can put you on fast track compared to the mass who are driven by goals of others.

Reality

When we know the reality it usually hurts. Earlier we know that it would be easier to make course correction to utilize remaining time.

The reality is our education prepared us for being an employee. It is decorated that way. Go to school, get good grade, get a job, life would secure and you will be happy. True, but it is a very limited aspect of living life.

What education we need is developing ourselves as persons who actually face the world with lot more enthusiasm, determination, creativity and willingness to showcase his or her individuality.

This has been missing in most of the professional learning we have taken. Question comes now, it is whose responsibility to learn the missing part? And you know the answer well.

As long as we blame others for the circumstances that we are in, we have become victims of the situation. A leader is one who takes ownership and responsibility to make those things work, which matters to him most. This mindset is essential to enjoy life and the glory it can offer as part of any individuals journey.

This a hidden aspect of life. Understanding it is not as easy as you have read it. You may not be able to appreciate victimized thinking on what harm it can make to individuals, until you realize that you have become part of it. This can happen in life or in career.

In fact we cannot behave very different in work or personal life or in any other given situation. Most of the time one may ignore saying I will take care of it when it is essential. An Approach towards a problem, treating it as a trivial one, but soon it becomes a habit in other areas too and we allow ourselves to become part of it.

Objective thinking is important; as if observed by a third party who is not influenced by the emotions involved in the situation. Till one develops at it, it may be good to discuss with others to get their point of view of your problems or interests.

Work with a Senior

You did that when you were walking first time, when you learnt to ride a cycle or even learning a motor vehicle.

Quickly identify a colleague who can be available when needed and is ahead in the area of your career. A two or three years senior colleague can be helpful here. A person from another team or independent of the work you are involved, would be a better choice.

Learn from them on how and what part. The right approach towards working, understanding the problem, arriving at multiple solutions and the right way of handling the issues. They can guide you easily. Problems that you are facing and finding it difficult to handle, has been successfully overcame by them in their earlier stint.

These mentors can be useful in correcting your email language, approaching your boss and oral communication in the team. Each of them plays a big role in the career growth.

Everyone has options. To choose a particular situation or project assignment is not always at your hand. So putting yourself ahead every time when in a group situation make your view heard. Here 80:20 rule applies. 80 percent of the success starts with showing up.

Periodic mentoring sessions and attending available corporate trainings should be ardently pursued. Thinking only technical skills helps you progress, may be true in only for certain jobs say for research and development activities or activities of individual contribution. People skill matters when it comes to group activities.

Be humble enough to approach others for help. It does not mean everyone will be willing to give you a helping hand. But however this exercise has to be done by you. Continue it until you have couple of mentors for different areas of work and may be even for life.

Team Player

Success cannot be achieved in solo. You need to be good with people whom you work with and as well develop your individuality.

Ability to get along with people is a great skill. It does not mean you need to be submissive so that you become YES type always. Though some managers prefer YES type, who are ready to execute their ideas without questioning. What is required is developing ability to put across your view point in a manner acceptable by others, without hurting any ones sentiments.

Developing assertiveness in both walk and talk should be deliberately practiced. It does not come natural during critical time of the project. Havoc can arise in the team due to missing of a deadline or a functionality altogether. And you need to prove your point and why that approach was taken with respect to all the inputs provided. Without assertiveness there is no leadership.

You have played in teams during your college days and your aim was to win the tournament. Supporting each other and taking up the roles at different times was part of the game.

Same applies in the work place. You need to play different roles at different times so that you understand the nature of works done by different individuals in the team. Moreover it may be handy when a team member unable to attend office.

You may have a choice for certain kind of work. But while you understand the former and later portion of your task helps not only to do your part in an artistic way, it aids to produce error free work.

Being a team player helps to get to know many people. Over period of time these networking with individuals help to find better projects within the organization or even outside. These peers will grow to senior positions later as you do. Any good connect as individual will help in future. So don't burn a bridge.

Street Smart

When I say street smart, it a simple and straight forward understanding and doing a thing without much emphasis on theoretical way of doing it.

Getting educated in best of the campuses gives us a formal way of doing things. While dealing with people of different cadre it helps to understand what kind herd mentality prevailing in a particular segment. This knowledge helps to take advantage as well safe guard ourselves.

Rich Dad has shared a good example of making free cold sales calls for an NGO during the evening and weekend. It actually enhanced the performance of the sales calls that he need to make in day time at the organization.

Whoever fails most will learn to be ahead of it. This is how entrepreneurs are made and this mindset is essential to enjoy career and in life. If we hesitate to make mistakes then we are hindering our ability to progress

They say, if you help by opening the cocoon yourself and there by not allowing the larvae to struggle in order to go out of the shell; it will lose their strength in limbs to become butterfly. Their wings fails. This is not only for butterflies alone but for everyone. We gain strength through our struggle.

Being part of majority will not help for long time. Identifying your strengths and weakness is essential to accelerate growth and avoid pit falls. Develop questioning mentality within first and then with others. By asking a question we may appear stupid for a minute. But there is a longer risk if you don't learn to ask questions.

Financial Education

Financial education is about knowing how world of money operates. It is a language of money. Getting financially educated means knowing what are the different investment instruments available, how risk and reward are linked in the money world, what is my risk appetite etc.,

Invariably most of our efforts are linked to money some way or the other. There is a stage of leadership where one need to overcome temptations of money, position, popularity or anything. Once we stay wealthy enough to retain the life style we are used to, then we may to be not affected by opinions of those around us easily.

World is organized in such a way that until we make enough of it, be anything, a particular interest, one cannot get away from it. In subsequent chapter, we will learn in depth and make efforts to stay conscious of ourselves.

There are different avenues to make money. Through salary, self-employment, via business and then with investments. This is a four quadrant representation of income from Rich Dad.

Multiple ways of earning are essential in this generation and easily possible. Today world has shrunk and opportunities lays at global playground for a worthy talent. This means there is no job security, but ample security of opportunities. Individual requires financial security. Thinking job and financial security as same can be a trap. Job security is an illusion most of us carry until the day we are fired or handed over with a pink slip.

Best time to dig a well is when there is no fire yet.

Starting point is understanding the history of money, the way it operates globally. Know about interest rates, GDP, micro and macroeconomics on the big picture scale. At a minute level understand how our emotions comes in the way and blocks us becoming rich. Many a times I have come across situations where people are unable to cash up on an asset and enhance the life style or learning. Not to fall for such trap means being financially educated. Understand that our life is an opportunity to learn and become better human, all things we do should lead us to that goal, including money.

IT- A service provider Industry

While you join a IT service provider company for a technical role, you would invariably involve in following type of the projects. Development, testing or maintenance support. Even combination of these three variants. Applies to both infrastructure and applications projects. Activities involved would be similar both in infrastructure projects and application related project execution. Infra projects require setting up of hardware and network related configurations and then hosting applications which run on these infrastructure environment.

There are support systems built around the major business applications. These subsystem help analyzing and presenting business outcomes as understandable reports termed as data analytics in a nutshell.

Development projects involve coding work based on the technologies involved. An IT project work begins with system design, derived from customer requirements, high and low level technical and functional design, their documentation, coding, test plans and test cases. Project may undergo different frameworks for development like iterative, agile or DevOps model based. Finished solution undergo testing and hosting the solution, finally to go live for actual usage by the end users.

Banking application which we use via our smart phones can be a good example here. Developing them from scratch or as an enhancement to already existing IT Solution, would form nature of work.

Testing project involves, testing the to be launched solution or services before putting them on for live use. Code may be developed by your organization or from your competitors organizations. Customers generally give projects to different vendors depending on their expertise in those areas and to bring the competitiveness among the service providers to enhance the quality of the solution.

Once the solution developed, tested and hosted, there is now necessity to maintain that piece of code with respect to its performance, downtime, service upgrade, errors occurred while using the application etc. Here comes the support or maintenance related application support addressed by a ticket based help desk.

IT infrastructure related projects, which involves designing and setting up of the hardware environment required for hosting the end solution. It can also fall in the three categories mentioned earlier.

Each of these type projects carries different way of working and different quality process to be followed. So it may be good to know the big picture again. It can help you design your career while you are staring it, considering your basic inclination towards development, testing and support based activities.

There is no recommended way to begin the career based on the above categories. Each area has its level of challenges, depth and importance. Having experiences in all the three areas of projects will be an advantage as one grows in the career. Application and infrastructure knowledge can put you in a commanding position while you make your progress towards leadership.

Knowing technical basics right at the beginning of the career makes you strong as you progress. In fact, being a genius is about mastery over fundamentals.

Technology scope keeps varying along with technical development happening in the world. What is in the limelight now may altogether be different in next two or three years. Being constantly updated on technology is a minimum requirement to stay in the IT world.

While we discussed on the development, testing and maintenance model it can come with different technologies. Each technology helps in certain way. Microsoft and Java based application development are of broad classification. There are custom tools for development environment. There are already many vendors with proprietary software. Commercial off the shelf product which can be used for business purposes or organizational functions.

After gaining a fair familiarity with a technology and business functions, it is time to know different vendors involved in a particular segment. One can gain comparative knowledge which product would be preferred under what condition. Aligning your interest properly with technology area and work nature helps to become one of those 20 percent in your company.

Big picture thinking, ability to get in and out of the intricacies of a project, at different stages of it, helps one progress faster in career.

Smart working is all about doing contribution on the more valuable tasks of the project. Identifying and contributing to the high value items makes one career grow faster. Apart one has to gain good control on English typing and using arithmetic functions of MS excel application.

Understand Organization

If you understand how your organization works then you have understood a major area. Because most of the businesses function in a similar way. Including your customers to whom you are working for. While you are trying to understanding your organization you would come across different areas of operations.

Here are a few pointers which can help.

- Start understanding the organization chart. It depicts who heads what functions. It lists all departments/divisions which are there in the organization.

- It supports big picture thinking and to know where to reach out within the organization. Helps to know where do you want to contribute in future years.

- At sub level understand project team organization. Which is the starting point since you can relate quickly how your contributions are added on at the value chain.

- Development team is like production department or earlier termed shop floor.

- Quality process defines how a particular activities should carried be out for optimum results. Examples like, code development will have code walkthrough and code reviews steps. Testing will have test cases to execute, testing sample data for dry run etc.

- Human resources department takes care of employee welfare, hiring and exit.

- Corporate finance department takes care of legal money matters, and there is public relations and media support teams.

- Training and skills enhancement department works on both technical and management related trainings required for employees.

- COE's center of excellence, works with a particular technology and having a research and development wing.

- Marketing team, develop the marketing strategy for showcasing the capabilities on technical and business transformation cases done earlier. Marketing team participate at different forums, national and international and helps in lead generation which sales team can cater to.

- Sales team works towards selling the products and services of a company.

- Administration department takes care of facility management and logistics related activities for getting employees to work place and catering facilities at office.

Enterprise Resource Panning

Enterprise resource planning software is set of business modules put together as one bundle. ERP software comes with different technologies and business modules required for running effective functioning of the organization electronic way.

Modules like, sales and marketing, human resources, accounting, , customer relationships, production, inventory, books keeping, legal compliance and many more. These modules can be tailor made to particular industry. ERP has ability to define the business process involved in the particular company to suit their needs by customizing it.

Since you have understood the organization chart and different departments involved. By going through the ERP software architecture and its functions at a broader level, one can also gain quick big picture view on how organization functions.

There are different levels of ERP's for different levels of businesses sizes. So take simple business ERP there are online ERP for trial, go through those module and map them to the business which your organization has. This helps you to a great extent in understanding what all happens in an organization and appreciate it.

Sooner you will find you have better advantage with bigger thinking since nobody around you usually thinks that way. This helps you to grow yourself faster in the organization.

|3|

LEARN AS MUCH

Best way to predict future is to create it
- Peter Drucker

Begin with end in Mind

You are going to spend major portion of your life in the corporate offices. It should be enjoyable, be supportive in growth and learning as an individual. It should not hinder your joy nor the contentment of having contributed daily at your best.

When this does not happen because of the culture at office you are in or by the people you are surrounded with or because of your own mental make-up, then work becomes a burden and not a source of joy.

I have seen people who don't want to make any one unhappy, plays a safe game and end with nothing as an individual. I have come across people who are so busy and those who don't even have time for their own development, even while they are free.

With the period of time they turn out to be negative source spreading harmful thoughts around.

I have come across people who are strikingly intelligent and focused. They grow in career with an astonishing speed, they are few and countable.

By now you more or less getting clarity of what is happening in the organization and how well it is getting coordinated completely You know where your role contributing to the big picture. If you still don't understand it after few years at work, then take time and effort to understand this on priority. People who knows where they are going usually reach.

Abroad Career

Lot of people in junior management prefer abroad career. They are excited about working at different cultures and places.

If you get a chance to do so, take it up or even pursue it ardently. Early career years at abroad can turn you as professional faster. It can work as an opportunity to get familiar and learn how things are professionally set at different countries. While at abroad learn keenly how business are being run and how it is organized to the minute level. This can be very handy to you while you work for yourself at later stage of your career.

You may note striking cultural difference with how people focus on professional and personal life. In developing countries, most consider work as life. In western countries they look work as means to live their life. That can be evident if you observe the way they plan vacation and how many times in a year. Planned vacation works as a refresher to refocus on the work with renewed spirit.

Developed countries have systemized every element of the society. Transport, water, electricity and there is no chance left for unknown. Such robust administrative system, lack in the developing countries. Learning how to systemize the business and social circumstances is a good input for the beginner visiting for working in other countries. Many a times, such differences encourage lot of people to settle down there, as it gives good life experiences.

Learning from those experiences and implementing them in your home land would be much more of value. This thinking has to be developed while we pursue our interests.

Ralph Waldo Emerson puts, *'human mind, once stretched by a new idea, never returns to its original dimensions'*. After working abroad ones thinking will vastly differs. Most important is how to utilize the expanded conscious in a right direction.

MBA Time

Many of you would have taken up job as stop gap arrangement or to have hands-on before moving to management studies. Doing management course from reputed colleges helps. You start developing yourself as a professional. MBA changes your mindset and the approach towards business.

Right time to do MBA is between 3 – 5 years of career experience. Earlier to 3 years it may be difficult to know, how business runs and about people mindset. Three years' time period will give you enough experience if you are focused on what is that you are intended to do with your career.

Later than 5 years, it may be difficult since your stake in life and at work would have increased significantly. Your mind set may not support day long studies that a good management school requires. Finish it early if you are inclined towards it.

Doing executive MBA can be handy. I advocate this approach because of the quality of students you meet. In a repute executive in-class room run courses you see people from middle management, senior management sponsored by the organizations. With quality of group discussions, case study debates and leadership qualities witnessed, will amplify one's learning. Considering the above MBA in distance or online mode will be difficult to cater these needs.

As a technical person one work at the details of the project without necessity of understanding the big picture view. A good 1 year course would be sufficient to build big picture thinking natural in yourself if you are a serious student. A 2 or 3 years course helps for average students. If your specialization in MBA complements on the area of experience you carry then learnings will be more powerful.

With family business background, you may pursue normal abroad MBA, since you already have a platform to play once you finish your course. Most employers look for cost effective solution, local MBA students are affordable easily and these students may stick to the job longer compared to students from the colleges of repute.

If you are not inclined for MBA you can still get those ideas with self-study by referring to case studies of Harvard Business School. Supplement it by reading the right management, business and self-help books. It helps to develop managerial thinking. However, a two years business course will invariably put you in that mindset and there is concrete shift in thinking taking place naturally.

Changing Jobs

This way is popularly practiced for increasing ones salary. Changing jobs every 2 – 3 years or even earlier. If your idea to make more money in short run and keep yourself satisfied with that aspect of life, then this is a good approach.

I have often found people who do that are financially successful and technology inclined. They would not have focused developing themselves in other aspects. While having only goal of money making through job can lead to lot of stress and compromise on leadership qualities.

Aspiring leaders can focus working for a shared goal, keeping mission more than the individual. This is possible by sticking to a particular organization for longer term and understanding its culture. One start developing respect towards greatness of the organization. Any emotional attachment to the organization or a particular brand does not help.

If your skills are not in demand then organization don't keep you and pay. Understanding this aspect helps individual to avoid shocks and resentment. Changing job can be one way , other way can be consciously pursue individual growth while working at a single company for longer a duration.

I have observed people who spend time for their development becomes more valuable over time. Their capacity to add value to the business increases, hence their income. People can choose what works and what matters to them.

A rolling stone gather no moss.

Certifications

In IT professional world certification matters. It makes interviewer comfortable to take a positive decision on your resume compared to the other resumes on hand.

Certification touches all gamut of the technical details which may not be used in the project we work at. It helps to know other possibilities of arriving at a a solution which may be better. Both in terms of ease of development and security concern it can address.

Getting certified ahead of others in popular technologies can get you lot of options inside the organization as well outside. It shows that you are on top of the technical trends and driven towards such development.

While technical certification focuses on the technical aspect of doing certain activities using the product. It also enhance the product knowledge and its usage.

There are business domain certifications. For a business analyst role domain certifications matter most. It shows they have industry standard knowledge on the process involved in that area. Be it banking or capital market or any manufacturing industries, etc.,

Toast Master

Toast master international is a nonprofit organization with self-sustaining business model. Organization is about teaching public speaking and for developing leadership in individuals.

Most of the organizations have their corporate TM Club in their campuses. There are community clubs which are for those who are not part of corporate.

Toast master organization has been doing wonderful service and effective progress over last ninety years. If you have a chance to get onto it go and do it on priority. It will teach you how to speak in front of public and stay strong on your thoughts. TM clubs have a very formal learning process in a formal environment which enables you to be a better speaker. It has both communication and leadership tracks.

You can visit a nearby club understand its structure and way it functions. People can attend the meetings as guest and then decide to become a member of a club for very nominal fees. I urge you to take this opportunity at the very first instance without thinking anything, it will be the wisest investment you are doing on yourself.

I remind Franklins remark, - '*an investment is the knowledge always pays you the best interest*'

You are responsible to your growth. Not your boss or the organization. They may show you the way, but you have to walk through to get those experiences for yourself. Having a mentor and following a known paths for self-development helps immensely.

Dale Carnegie has said '*ability to speak is a short-cut to distinction* '

One day your realize all the investments you have made in yourself, will reflect in the confidence and in the way you operate. Ability to influence large number of teams, in giving them clear direction and in driving business results with human values.

Entrepreneur Mindset

Entrepreneur mindset is about being creative. Developing on questioning the status quo, on improving the way which is being done currently and arriving at a thinking which is positive, conductive to growth and experimental based.

This begins with individuals. It does not need any qualification and experience. It needs an inquisitive mentality which questions and comes with an satisfying answers.

Right way is to start understanding why things are in the way they are and not in any other way; you start developing on entrepreneur mind set. Innovations at all levels are encouraged by corporates. Working on this approach which can put you on to limelight and make you stand out of the crowd easily.

Once you are out of crowd, leaders recognize your potential and can give you an offer to do better. Make sure your uniqueness and individuality is in the design and the way you present your ideas to the leaders, who may help define your future.

Entrepreneurship teaches you to develop risk taking abilities, finding uniqueness in you and collaborative way of working. Entrepreneurs should be ready to work at all levels. They don't wait for others to join in or they don't wait for that perk approval. They start where they are and with what they have. A very important aspect in any business and one has to develop that consciously.

While you pursue your dreams, you find it usually adds energy. It teaches you to be self-motivated and does not need a boss to define or monitor what you do day today. Coming to making investment on your ideas, exercise caution on the for being it spent wisely. It may be good to have a constant thinking, i this the best return on this investment I can get?, what is the opportunity cost involved here, considering the time, money, energy and emotions being put on particular idea or a cause.

Over period of time employees may observe that those daily routine, defined tasks, monitoring systems and even false hopes by superiors, all can deplete ones energy in exerting his or her best day today.

Antidote can be developing, entrepreneurs mindset. Identify and involve in the work which energizes you in the office. That is individual's responsibility. You cannot blame others or situation you are in anytime, it's just an outcome of choices you have taken in the past. Remember the power choice topic or revisit it.

Designations

In IT world designations are fancy. Many a times organizations offer different designations to satisfy and retain the talents. It may or may not fully depict the nature of your work. However if you are growing as person in your career and knowledge then this aspect should not matter much. Consciously don't allow titles to dilute your mind towards a positive or negative feelings.

My suggestion don't fall for designation, they help creating a hallow around the person. Leadership is about who you are and what actions you do. If you are waiting for right designation to project your activities to the world then you are relaying on the positional leadership. Less effective in the knowledge era.

Designations can make tremendous impact on the people when associated with popular brands. It can act in multiple ways, including the effect of how you feel about yourself. In reality, it may take a while in career to understand that it is an ink on your visiting card. Nothing more, nothing less.

If you have a choice to choose the designation, then choose the one which is different from the lot. One which inspires you and gives an opportunity to tell more about your activities while you exchange your business cards. Remember it's your role which add meat to your career growth as an individual. It is important to know this difference at first five years of your career. It can make whole lot of differences and accelerate your growth.

A serious question. Consider your designation versus person you are. Most of the people gets associated with the title they hold very dear to their heart. Always ask question what you really are? this goes without title, without company names associated with you. A harsh reality is always better than the false projection of self.

You are unique because of what you do, not because how you are called or what you have in your procession. Those things can move away from anybody anytime.

Appraisal Process

Good you think you have completed all of your exams. Reality is it is not over yet. It starting again with your employment. Somebody at the end of every quarter or half yearly or annually will rate your performances against a bench mark on which your increments or promotions in the career are decided.

Appraisal is important in order to find the top performers within the organization. Performance will be based on the goals and objectives you have agreed upon at the beginning of year. It should develop a healthy competitive spirit to showcase your uniqueness and contributions made to the business.

While the Goals and objectives for your role is templated within the organization, you have liberty to customize them according to your project or work nature. It is important that you device your G & O according to your growth plan you have in mind. It is suggested to go through all the G & O published in the organization intranet, so that you understand what kind of responsibilities are expected out of what roles or designation.

Always have access to immediate next two level role descriptions and corresponding G & O handy enough to refer often. It helps to know are you growing in the direction which you are intended.

Many feel appraisal process are not seen from employee perspective, but from the organizations view or your supervisor view of you. Hence it is important to consider this as a formal process which defines your growth in the corporate ladder. Reviewing G & O every month is an important step that everyone can follow irrespective of the career stage

Develop an ability to look appraisal as a tool to showcase your contribution. Accepting the limitation of being appraised by the supervisor's point view should encourage you to show case your leadership abilities boldly.

Perception of supervisor about you will clearly reflect in the outcome of an appraisal. Because when it comes to pay you back to equal to your contribution, lot more dimension may appear, which otherwise would not have seen before. Be prepared for that. We learn more about it in the inner circle topic at a later chapter.

Retaining your perception about yourself amidst career turmoil is important. It should be cultivated consciously.

A three or five scale ratings are usually practiced in the corporates with expectation that last 5 to 10% rated people need to look jobs outside. Sufficient time and improvement plans are provided to prove oneself as competent and skilled, this works as a second chance.

A PERSONAL LIFE STAGE

This section describes your personal life while you are carried on with your junior management job.

Considering that you are single and would have enough time for yourself to identify your interests and pursue them wholeheartedly.

Work on understanding who you are, whom you want to be, identifying what makes you unique and valuable to others. Take enough time to figure out that. It will immensely help to achieve your life goals and moreover for unprepared surprises which life offers. Haziness here can be costly both to life and on pocket at later stages.

Once you are clear on who you are, then you are ready to identify what kind of personality can be your ideal partner.

Try finding a partner whom you know and have spent some time together in family, friends circles, education, common interest areas or at work. Once both are sure what is that they are looking for in life and in each other company; it is time to think ahead. Finding similarities helps and knowing dissimilarities may help better on how to complement each other on path of progress; concept of soul mates makes sense that way.

You may figure out your personality type working with mentors, through psychological tests so that you know your hidden personality and to be clearer on your true aspirations.

Assuming somebody out there, to bring you happiness can be a pit fall. Putting enough time to understand what kind of life you wish to lead helps to find a right partner. It's worth the struggle.

Your goal of becoming a leader begins with taking ownership for your personal life. Learn and arrive at your personal and at family vision. Rewrite it until it becomes crystal clear. Most of the time early success requires ideal situation at personal front.

ACTION EXERCISE

A Typical Day

- This section is addition to the previous winning practices and same applies in future sections too.

- In knowledge era people who knows a clear path would achieves it faster. Knowledge can be accessible easily however having a reach to a role model can be real progress booster.

- Degree of street smartness matter most.

- Average work hours per week is 40. Most of the organization track your on floor hours in premises for finding average productivity, compliance with the norms etc.,

- If you are staying in metro cities travel would take additional 2 hours on average to commute to office

- Keeping yourself fresh and energetic while at work matters. Build your personal habits and staying near to office helps

Learning Areas

- Read a book every month

- Learn to organize your life, you are sculpting a master piece out of raw you. It needs efforts and devotion

- Learn to go with flow as well keeping eye on your individuality.

- Know that focus on one area comes at an expense of neglecting other areas

Recommendations

- Start identifying your role models. Role models can differ for different areas of interest. Learn to seek guidance, your focused questions will be appreciated by your mentors.

- Good written and oral communication always pays

- Ability to speak clear in accent helps a lot and leaves the listener with positive impact.

- Staying physically fit and mentally alert is the first step to achieve more in same 24 hours.

Read following books

- Rich dad poor dad - Robert kiyosaki

- Enterprise resource planning demystified. – Alexis Leon

- Investing in Financial Markets Is Not a Rocket Science - Balaji Rao DG

- The Secret – Rhonda Byrne

- Get paid more and promoted faster – Brian Tracy

PART III

MIDDLE MANAGEMENT

NAVEEN CHANDRA

Focus Area

This section discusses about what one has to focus to learn as part of middle management career. Typical age groups 30 – 40 years.

As one progresses towards middle management focus has to become two-fold. Earlier it was to take care of his career shaping. Now along with it one has to have the ability to give directions to others. To retain talents and align them towards goal of the project and organization.

Not all prefer managing people as part of their career growth. Some may prefer to stick to core technology area and move towards path of technical solution design, architecture and specializing with certain technological areas or products. Their main focus would be to give technical direction while designing a multilevel solution for business needs.

Whoever wishes to handle a team of people be technical or functional experts; skill to handle a team is essential. It is a learnable skill. First level of leading others will always start with the ability to leading one self.

Middle management career puts you a strong hold on business and people. It prepares you rightly for next level of management, provided you are interested in that. Most of the folks may not wish to take up the challenges of senior management. They feel their focus is needed at personal life. Sometime being contended with the progress they have achieved in terms of career responsibilities.

Clear understanding of self as an individual, building on the strengths gained so far and being open enough to learn. These qualities helps to identify the avenue for a unique contribution, which only you can make. It is a royal road for a fulfilling career and job satisfaction.

Let's go through those ideas.

|4|

CROSS SKILLING

Person trying to catch two rabbits, catches none – Socrates.

Management

Rightly using the resources available towards attempt to meet the business goals. In simple terms it has to do with getting work done. These resources are predominantly man power in I.T industry. Managing people in terms of their unique contribution, right blend of experiences, bring the optimum cost structure for the project execution team, arrive at the solution within the allocated time and budget are the primary responsibilities of a project manager.

It also includes planning ahead for people for different stages of the project, to scale up and down the team sizes during the course of the project duration.

Customers hail from different business domain, be it banking, securities and capital markets, health care, life sciences, manufacturing, oil and gas etc. These domain segregation are important. A few roles like functional experts, business Analysists are specific to domain and they help to convert the business process to the software programing language.

People don't learn by reading subjects. Most of the learnings happen when we do things on hands. People who are in demand are the people who have undertaken similar tasks earlier. It saves time, efforts and money required to bring up the team to the effective level required for the solution delivery.

However, same principle may not work always in IT. Sometimes it would be easier to teach a novice who is open to learn and ready mold to the ways of working which is needed. Hence we see large number of people being recruited from the campus with a fixed commitment to serve the company for a few years at a stretch.

Verticals & Horizontals

Vertical division helps to manage the business across different industry segments where IT development and support are needed. Segments like – Utilities, power, water, oil and gas, engineering design, manufacturing, aerospace, banking, cyber securities, securities and capital markets and many more.

Customer belonging to particular segment will be assigned to a vertical. Verticals keep history of different customers served in that domain and have the responsibilities to gain the insights into that segment of business. They stay ahead of the knowledge required to implement solutions for those particular business areas.

Horizontals refer to technology specific areas related to a particular vendor. Say like Microsoft, Adobe, SAP, IBM related technologies. These technologies specific horizontal group focuses on creating prototypes and to showcase model solutions and developing those competencies in employees. Horizontals considers the latest technological trends.

Preparing for certifications, getting training for staff, partnership with vendors, creating center of excellence, giving roadmap for employees who pursue their technical career growth, all these forms a primary goals of a horizontal.

Functional Learning

Business analyst and functional experts come with knowledge and experience of a particular business segment. People from banking background would be knowing what all steps are involved in a cheque clearing process. Similarly experts from securities and capital market come with knowledge on how trading settlement cycle happens.

While arriving at a business solution or for maintaining the existing business solutions, functional experts are needed to understand the business processes involved. Hence required training and hands on the system allows them to provide an expert opinion on the system design level. Other factors like security checks, process flow and approvals are considered. Subsequently, what all sub-areas for a particular transaction including, the pre and post conditions for a proper execution or roll the back to normalcy, in case of a transaction failure are explored. All these information should be of interest for functional experts or business analysts.

Even within the organization, knowing how and where to seek expert opinion matters. It applies both on technical feasibility and functional areas coverage in the solution. Coupled with setting task priorities and engaging all members in the teams should be of interest for a project manager who owns the entire solution delivery responsibility.

Process Orientation

Developing an appreciation for producing quality goods or services should be every professionals basic intent. IT industry has come out with different process models or frameworks for developmental projects. Started with traditional waterfall model, it begins with design till testing in a sequential way, there is agile methodology, which has small stories and interactive way of developing the code for faster time to market and then the DevOps where both development and maintenance are handled together for a amplified solution delivery.

Cost of quality, finding an error at a later stage of the solution can be expensive affair for an IT service provider. To change a feature of a solution going back and redoing is difficult because of the cost, effort and time factors. Customers come with penalty clauses for not delivering the solution in a timely and with agreed level of functions. Without stringent quality orientation development of product or service is not very useful.

Marketing, Sales and Presales

Marketing is about positioning your product or services in the right customer segment. Identifying opportunities, which can be cashed up with a product or service fitting conveniently in the gap in market place offers which already flooded with various competitors' products. It is a study by itself. Creating the collaterals and preparing media kits for sharing, participating in national and international exhibitions and answering visitors queries and concerns can reveal lot about market sentiments.

All the execution works in terms of development, maintenance and testing is possible only if you have a customer. Hence highly skilled and competitive people are needed in sales, who understand and connect with customers in a right manner. Sales teams with domain knowledge would meet the customer and arranges for subject matter expert and presales team to involve in the discussion to gain overall understanding of a customized solution need.

Alternatively organizations who is in need IT of solutions would float a 'Request for proposal(RFP) or information (RFI) for major IT service providers. Tailor made bids will be submitted by these IT service providers for the seeking organization. Organization would go through similar other RFPs submitted by different vendors. Checks on pros and cons and then awards the bid a particular vendor. Terms and conditions, penalty clauses and payment cycles are discussed.

This may go through few rounds of discussion or creating a prototype of a service or a solution. Sometimes organizations will like to try hands on with one line of business before opting for its entire operations or multi country rollouts.

For taking over the IT support from the incumbent service provider, there are set of procedures. That includes doing due diligence, working as secondary support and then take over primary support. Generally these transition exercises are done in different phases or waves and handed over.

This typically takes 2 – 3 months of effort again based on the size of the support required. And can span more if it's a very huge business support requirement.

In any business, sales and marketing areas need 80% focus, energy and efforts. Otherwise we would have the best quality product with fewer buyers or even no buyers. Sales team though a very small in number but they get the business to work upon. Sales team are highly incentivized and are driven by achievement targets.

Most of the senior management team in corporate comes with sales background. Once you are familiar with the project execution, look for business development roles. People who wish to grow faster in the career should quickly aim to move to sales team.

Professional Etiquettes

These relates to dressing, overseas culture, food eating, clothing and many more. They are required. Following them makes people to understand that you know what you are doing. It helps to relate to you easily. In simple words birds of same feather flocks together. Spend quality time to pick up these basic in dressing etc., so that your appearance is a welcome in the environment you are related.

Since you are exposed to international business, cross culture etiquettes becomes essential. All these are required until you develop rapport with your customers, colleagues and business partners. Once the rapport is established by proving your knowledge and skills, scope for little deviation possible. However basics should be in place for most of the formal meetings or gathering. As one grow in corporate career, he or she can consider personnel branding to showcase a uniqueness as an individual. It helps you retain your individuality and quick recognition among the peers.

Basic Management lessons

For traversing on management path, it is important to understand stand a few universally accepted management theories. This comes handy as they are referred often in the decision making. You can get these information in your MBA study or by going through business management books.

Listed a few classical theories in brief format.

- **Parato principle 80/20 rule** - states that, for many events, roughly 80% of the effects come from 20% of the causes. Vilfredo Pareto showed that approximately 80% of the land in Italy was owned by 20% of the population.
  You may observe 80% progress you achieved in your life can be attributed to 20% of best practices you follow. Many research has been done on this principle and it works taking a rough approximate. One can use this principle at work and at personal life.

- **90/10 rule**
  It states that: 10% of life is made up of what happens to you, and 90% of life is decided by how you react. It was popularized by Stephen Covey. You may see top 10% in any industry makes most of the money as observed by Rich Dad.

- **Maslow's theory of hierarchical needs**.
  As motivational theory, Abraham Maslow puts forth five layered human needs in the shape of a pyramid.
  Starting at the bottom of pyramid we find.

  Physiological need – food, cloth shelter
  Safety needs – physical, environmental, jobs
  Social needs – belongingness, community, respect
  Esteem needs – confidence, USP, recognition, position
  Self-actualization –contentment, social service, acceptance

  It helps to figure out our individual state of progress and wants in life. We can also use this principle to understand the general human nature, tendencies and its evolvement at different levels of maturity. Though it is not necessary to be in that order always. We may see a self-actualized person without basic needs and vice versa.

- **Herzberg's two factor theory of motivation**
  Herzberg says, in job there are factors which gives job satisfaction. He categorized those factors as hygiene and motivators.
  Hygiene – Pay, policies, work conditions, benefits and job security
  Motivators – recognition, promotion, responsibility and meaning.

- **Theory X and Theory Y**
  Douglas McGregor suggested two aspects of human behavior at work. He termed, negative views of individuals – theory X and positive view termed theory Y.
  X Factor – person shuns responsibility, resist change, requires monitoring
  Y Factor – self-motivated, external control not necessary, skilled.

- **Time management matrix.**
  Stephen Covey puts across 2 X 2 matrix method towards time management. This considers Urgent and Important tasks.

	Urgent	Not Urgent
Important	crisis, emergencies	planning, prevention, improvement
Not important	Interruptions Telephone	Time wasters TV Channels hopping

Good mangers spend more time in quadrant 2 and follows best practices often. Ben Shahar's happiness model can be referred here as modern theory.

Industry Overview

In the beginning pages we have understood the importance of choosing an industry and not a job. Choosing a job is a short term solution for a long term problem. Choosing industry invariably make you think career wise.

Since you have done that, it is time to understand that in detail. Go through the complete activities as IT service provider industry does. There will be a gamut of areas when looked in detail. So your study include all these areas. Voice support, Business process support, IT applications, IT infrastructure and many more. You get into details of these sub segments based on your interest. Then understand which companies are active in those segments, their focus area, business, geographies spread and skill set their employees possess.

This kind of big picture thinking helps to broaden thinking and to decide on area of contribution. If you are clear then it is easier to design your career. You find research and management consultant like McKinsey, Gartner, Forrester and others. They produces industry segment reports, which give focus of the industry and possible future developments in that area. Specific company annual reports can give you more details of their business focus.

Great career do not happen by accident. If you are working with eminent organization, chances are that you would come across the best practices of that industry. It would be wise to target to get into the tier 1 level organizations in any industry. It helps you to focus on your career where all these research are made available in their intranet sites.

Thinking in terms of who are the major players, what are their market capitalization, owner lineage, understanding the organization's annual report, analyzing the trends and projecting into future to identify which industry segments may thrive. All these approach gives you a definite edge over your colleagues and can work as catalyst in your career.

|5|

MANAGING SELF

A Single conversation across a table with wise man is better than ten years of mere study of books - Henry Wards worth Longfellow

Self Help

When people know what they want, they usually achieves it and exceeds too. It is not easier to arrive at the clarity on what one really want in career and life.

As one proceeds with a corporate career one need to have lot more agility to achieve more in same 8 hours, that everyone has. To make that happen one need to develop himself a as a person of credibility, clarity and focus.

People who has these qualities are the ones who progress in the corporate. You can look at your two level above supervisors and observe their ability of working longer, to get into details, untiring focus, getting to a right solution. You may also note their ability to present different angles of a problem and probable solutions, moreover presenting the facts in an affirmative and decisive way. All these qualities in a person shows that he or she knows not only knows how to lead himself but also the business.

Giving directions to people, charting out their career map, conducting annual appraisals, communicate the status to stake holders, all these has to go into the skills to be picked up on your way of climbing the corporate ladder.

When you have a supervisor who can handhold you doing these things and making you sit next to him while solving the real business problems, it is a sure shot way of learning the management quickly.

As an alternative one can focus on the below pointers to ensure he or she is growing irrespective of the outside circumstances.

Clarity

Clarity precedes success. We have learnt that. Our education system has prescribed common subjects to all and may not consider individuality to any great extent. Though there are sufficient areas of learnings to consider.

The real need is to find out what is our passion all about. It means we need rework on ourselves first. Now it is up to our own interest to understand the importance of uniqueness which only you can offer.

Going forward we will lean how to narrow down to a goal which is conductive to growth as human. Base it on the innate strength we naturally has as an individual.

To gain clarity as individual, as a professional and finding our uniqueness is not an easy task. At each level of achievement and growth, one requires next level of clarity. There is always a room for learning. That's how mentoring and working with seniors whom you respect helps. This can be easily understood when you know best of the sports players still have their coaches to guide further in their career.

We have learnt it is the top 10% of any industry makes best of it. Then same way if we want to reach top 10% of where we are now, we need to distinguish ourselves from others by doing those things which only 10% does.

Having same skills, same qualification would not make one different from the crowd. How can we turn a situation to our own strengths and then play with it. Developing an ability to look the same situation from an angle where others are not able to do so easily. Technically termed as out of box thinking. Such qualities can make one a better professional as he or she grows in the career.

Writing down the questions like, who you are, what makes you unique and answering them over and again, will leads to clarity.

A Passion Test

I have observed people who have made it to the top level of their business or career, did not achieve it without being passionate about what they are doing today. Their passion fuels them when everything around them looks not encouraging. These individuals have learnt their way of keeping energetic toward what they wish to achieve.

Mr. Donald trump once said *'without passion you don't have energy and without energy you have nothing'*.

How do we know we are passionate or not?

Here are a few pointers, which I generally discuss in my corporate sessions.

- What you really enjoy doing
    You don't know how much time has passed since you have involved in that work you enjoy, you don't keep track of time

- What people say as your strengths
    Many times people will tell you, what you are doing is so good. which you might think it as a normal way of doing it.

- Are you ready to work for free
    Look for this hint. This is significant. If you can find this out you know what you are really about.

- You have done 24/7 and still want to do it more
    You never find it enough of doing the same thing over and again and never get bored off

- Creative juices flows naturally
    Your individuality comes out naturally without even making much efforts towards it

- Whom do you relate to.
    Sometime when you see a successful person or even a neighborhood business tycoon or simply one on television, suddenly you feel connected and say to yourself that you want to be one of them.

These pointers can reveal what is it that our passion is about. This can be used as a test over and again until we have the required clarity.

Values

The origin of your intention lies in your values. What you value most in your life. You will not be able progress further as leader if you don't spend time on yourself. Values work as moral compass and guide our endeavors in life.

Chalk out a personal journey, identify the mentors who can truly give you the direction without any bias. It is easier to figure out our values based on the way we react under pressure. These values stem from personal experiences, the way we were brought up and it gets established by the choices we make over years. Then there will be huge internal resistance to make any changes to it.

Start working on yourself with a journal. Analyze what kind of options you have taken in life. What kind of short cuts you have considered etc., List them and understand what was the thinking behind those actions. Don't even miss one choice you made in your life. Then try identifying a pattern in that. It would not lie. Make note of them. Accepting the ignorance is the starting point of learning.

You have started your inner journey. When you stop journaling your journey towards leadership stops. Don't let that happen, you have come so far in your growth and what is the point in dropping the ball now.

List them as much as you find, then identify the core values out of them, which you are not ready to part with. Like you would rather die than give up your value, which is an extreme example!

Sooner you start realizing invariably your values are playing beneath the choices you have made so far in life. Be it professional, playing in sport league, the spirit behind each of your achievement, all can give you a hint. Observe closely what was important to you at that point of achievement in that significant goal of your life.

When your core values are disturbed you don't find peace in your endeavors. Now look at the values which you would like to have in you in the future and then work towards it.

Values are basically our choices and it mean it can be changed. Changing values would not give immediate results, but lead to a personal transformation over time, which is worth striving for.

A sample value list.

Accountability	Determination	Leadership	Service
Ambition	Enthusiasm	Love	Timeliness
Boldness	Fairness	Loyalty	Vision
Balance	Freedom	Originality	Intuition
Calmness	Generosity	Selflessness	Teamwork
Challenge	Honesty	Simplicity	Discipline

Wheel of Life

With the wheel of life, big picture thinking should become natural. It encompasses all round details in a nut shell. When we have such thinking naturally, then we don't do anything half away through. We focus for completeness.

Having an understanding that we have limited time in this world to make difference is a good starting point. Take a holistic view of your life. A 360 degree view. Below figure is with 4 quadrants. You can mention basic life needs here. Health, Wealth, Family and Career.

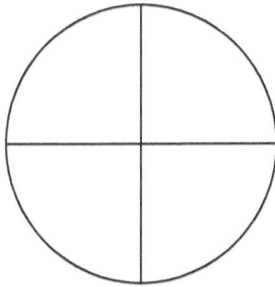

When you divide a circle with eight part and name each portion as part of your life and you track them. viz. Health, wealth, family, career, social, legacy, hobbies and spirituality.

Consider each spoke from the center to a point of circle. Treat it as 100% of a desired achievement in that particular area of life. Now mark a point on that spoke what is your current progress in that area. Example health. Likewise, do for each part. And once you connect all the dots which is your current progress, check is that still looks like a circle.

The diagram, you get can reveal you that, have you considered seriously all areas of your life or not. If you want to have some more dimensions of the life to be tracked then add them as a spoke in the diagram. If you are comfortable with lesser spokes, you can try that out.

Start with having a clear picture on those areas of life which matters most for current situation. Also understand how you want to allocate time for those areas of life. Reviewing it often, as frequently as once in three months can help to gain lot of control on our life.

Vision

With wheel of life approach, one can be practical about developing a compelling vision for entire life. Chances that one may even decide, that if I achieve certain goals of life, then I call my life as successful. While that is easier to consider and operate that way, however it makes better sense when we consider the complete life.

Vision is about seeing a probable future in the mental eye. Since our mind thinks as images, it may be good idea to have a collage of pictures that inspires. Seeing them often helps to recollect ones vision for achievement and experiencing similar things in his or her life. Having clear vision helps to achieve it faster. And it can imprint a concrete image in the subconscious mind. One need to *see* it before seize it.

Once we have a clear vision on what we want to be in the career and in life, we are ready for process of visualization. It's a conscious mind exercise of seeing and feeling with emotions, about achieving the goal result in a positive way. If one can visualize the steps towards the final goal, it would be even more effective in materializing it.

Visualizing talks about thinking and acting as if you have achieved your vison. A step by step thinking and feeling in the mind that we are already experiencing the results we want. Do this exercise for a brief period of time every day. It creates a subconscious impression within our mind and thereby help us to pick up those points during conscious hours naturally and act upon it easily.

Once we have these things in place, we can also have a written form of them along with or without pictures like a mission statement. This act as a guiding principle when the moment of choice comes and confuses us. As one progress in life these vision and mission statement can be improved based on the clarity one achieves.

A personal SWOT exercise helps to reveal individual strengths. One can then focus on developing on those strengths. And avoid working on projects related to your weak areas. It may not help to give as much results compared to working on a project where your strengths are in use.

It's natural to build on what is easily available within us. When we work on our natural talents and enhance them with hard work, we can grow faster compared to picking a skill where we are average and working hard to make it first grade. It may not bring the success one aspires.

Goals

Once you are clear about your passion, your values, it is now time to derive a structured way of arriving there via goals. Without proper plan of action most of the vision remain as dreams.

Goals make us focus. When we focus on one thing other things will suffer, this is natural. Good idea is to segregate your time into three buckets. I observed most of the successful people follow similar structure.

- 50% of our time, focus, energy and effort should go to maintain those items which are already there with us. (Health, wealth as per wheel of life etc.)

- 25% of time, energy and focus allocate to new projects, innovation, future related and for continuous education.

- 25% of time for recreation and enjoyment. We need to have time and ability to enjoy what you have already accumulated.

This time management approach or division can be on daily basis or one day fully in a week for particular activities or devote some seasons of the year. It is up to individuals based on what works for your present condition. An essential step to go to next level of achievement.

SMART Goals

You know them. Specific, measurable, attainable, realistic and time bound.

State your goal in a single sentence with the above points taken care. When you write down your goals it creates an impact on your subconscious mind, stating this is most important to consider. Repetition and re-writing down makes it concrete. So arrive at goals which are 90 days, 6 monthly, one, two and three years till 5years.

Know that what part of the wheel of life you are addressing with this kind of structure. Over a period of time with proper goal setting, execution and tracking you develop ability to do more with less time. You start feeling you are in charge of yourself than anyone or anything else.

Former CEO of General Electric, Jack Welch has said, '*either we will be in number 1 or 2 of the industry segment we are in; otherwise we don't do business*'.

Stephen Covey has remarked, '*Goals can be 1 or 2*'. These statements indicate that, we need to be tremendously focused to progress ahead with our goals.

Assessments

Assessments help us to check where we are with respect to our leadership growth. It may be a good idea to go through the them once in a year or two. They are provided by most learned on the human psychology and leadership. It helps to understand and correct our path towards leadership, right way.

Here I have mentioned popular leadership assessment methods which are widely used. There may be better methods, beginner can still go ahead with these. Suggest taking same assessment again after a few years and it does indicate your growth properly.

- Mayer and Briggs type indicator

- DISC profile

- Strength finder

- John Maxwell's leadership assessment

These indicators help to understand our self. When somebody gives us feedback, we may not take it or like it as it is. But with self-assessments we don't fall into that trap. These result helps to bring out what is not visible part of us. Moreover to control what negative traits which one might be displaying without his or her knowledge.

As you establish yourself in leadership thinking, start identifying those leadership styles which suites more to your innate nature. You would be able check those pattern, with some of these indicators. It helps actually one to grow up to next level leadership. And you will start appreciating these indicators.

One can also begin with free leadership assessment tools available at www.mindtools.com

Crisis in Job

Without saying about crisis in job, a career book will be incomplete. Lot of people drag themselves to office due to compulsion and necessities. Like all life areas, one may be subjected to negativity by the situation. Some may be real and few more are imaginary. Because we are not able to accept the facts as is and relay on the hope. Most of the time individuals wait for circumstance to rise up to his expectation, which rarely happens. If such things happens with career, it may lead to major disappointment in life as we spend most of our days at work.

In career one may often find that talent and hard work alone may not get the due recognitions. It requires getting along with the people. Understand that the human emotions are involved in any of the group decisions and it can vary.

Identify and focus on what is in one's control and improve oneself constantly. Developing as an individual who is capable of looking good in everything, matters most. This calls for affirmative actions, ready to convey feelings without emotions. Neither aggressive nor being submissive. One has to consciously develop this trait to be able to contribute unbiased.

Lot of times one may find that, people are not stable with their voice and views under pressure. And also by the expectations of their own and even by others. Nothing can be more divesting than this. When a negative situation prevails around us, we can use that as a learning lesson, to not to do the same way when we are in similar position in future. In that way any of the situations can be helpful for our growth as human.

Management consultant Peter Drucker wrote, *"the most important thing in communication is to hear, what isn't being said"*.

When we are surrounded with people we tend to become one of those. One need to be cautious of what he or she is becoming, knowingly or unknowingly. If you are in the company of survivors who do things as just necessary, those who are with narrow focus and self-centered view of the monetary benefit, then make efforts to figure that out on priority, soon or later we become one of them.

Office politics has to be accepted. More one delays and denies, longer would be the suffering. Finding the niche where you can play your heart out, is a necessary step to get the job satisfaction. Otherwise it will elude for life time.

People achieved great heights in career, earned tons of money, but somewhere they lost the meaning of life in the pursuit of so called the growth. I realized world has similar pattern whether it is corporate or business. I had begun with the belief that professionals carry right spirit and judgment.

Luckily, I did met leaders who made me understand these differences of human nature. Once understood this fact, one can reserve his or her endeavors towards a right direction. A leader keeps your best interest always in his heart. Does educate them in a manner where one can grow as an individual with courage and ability to share their views in an unbiased way.

If this quality develops in an individual he is heading in the right direction of growth and self-actualization. It requires hard work and recreating one's personality out of reality. Leadership involves identifying the gaps between who we are and what we project ourselves as and then make efforts to align ourselves rightly.

Emperor Marcus Aurelius' said. *'first to keep the unperturbed heart. And second to look in the eyes and know what it is.'*

Crisis in job helps our learning process and even probes us to understand the meaning of inner circle.

The Inner Circle

The concept of inner circle is about people who are closely connected on the purpose of business and vision. Over time it will behave like a protective circle to retain the maximum benefits to the people who are inside. These people will understand the core purpose of running the business activities with an eye on personal agenda.

When it comes to portraying to the social circumstance it comes out in a socially accepted way. However there is pitfall in getting to something which has to be masked in some way or other, then that is not the right way of doing things. It's doing things right.

Normally it is the inner circle people who take decisions and leading on where the business should head towards. Here 90:10 rule may apply. Understanding this universal principle will help one to align with clear purpose and clarity. People do business with people they like and with people whose thinking matches. If this basis is not met, putting across your point however good it may be, it may not be taken for an action.

Once you are part of an inner circle, the rules which are made to manage others does not applies to you. You see such people progress faster in the career at the cost of compromised values. Over a period of time one may have everything of materialistic value, but deprived of inner satisfaction. Ability to do good for all involved, has gone away from thinking and it is completely replaced by narrow selfish motives. One will be limited with the thinking of self or of those who are in the inner circle.

This approach does not lead to leadership in true sense. Preparing a core team based on values and ethics are important. A good start for a business comes with onboarding of right set of people.

As a leader your responsibility lies in creating an environment where right thinking and openness forms the base of team work.

Thank you for Firing me

Job loss can hit anyone at any time. Accepting this fact, puts you in a position to consider that as an opportunity to your advantage.

You can look at how to retain the job. You can look at this as a break to relook at your priorities and the direction you are leading to in your life. It is your skills which gives you money. If you have a skill which is rare you are priced high. Constantly looking how to stay tuned with right skills, is every professional's responsibility.

Once you know your true worth and confident about your knowledge, you can be bold in your day to day work. It shows in the energy and creativity with which you do your work.

Having sufficient bank balance and ability to pay your monthly commitments gives you confidence and opportunity to explore. Achieving this stage is important before you get into a situation of job loss. I would recommend anyone to have Job loss fund going forward entirely not accessible for any other purposes. Best way to do that is by monthly contributing to voluntary provident fund.

Beauty of life is, if you accept anything with proper reasoning and judgement, you can learn a lot from that event. It can fuel your personal growth. Becoming emotional towards job, organization or on work contributions you have made, may make one suffer more in odd times like job loss.

You have learnt to see things objectively. Take your focus to the future, because that's where life is.

|6|

LEADING TEAMS

I have learned silence from the talkative, tolerance from the intolerant and kindness from the unkind; yet, strange, I am ungrateful to those teachers
Khalil Gibran

Team Spirit

While one has been leading him or herself successfully for quite some time then he or she is fit to lead others.

Lot of people are eager to go to next level of their profession without being prepared enough for it. They think they are fit because of a few past successes, it does not make one complete. One has to go through enough failures too; then the generosity required at higher level comes naturally. Such person can avoid inter team conflicts easily and can become role model to their juniors. I suggest one take to a deeper thinking on this aspect.

To be successful in a career, regardless of title or position, focus on developing leadership skills. It is not the position which makes

one leader, it's not even the good intension of leading. It's about actions what you are doing and not doing defines you as a leader.
Leading means ability to give direction to teams work. Ability to forecast the time and efforts required to complete a task, a basic skill. It requires *big picture* thinking of where all it affects and on how to scale up team in coming quarters. We will learn more of it as go we further.

Team Work

Together everyone achieves more. Team can be a set of people working towards a common goal. When different people come into a project, they are there for different reasons. Their primary focus would be nature of work, alignment with their personal aspirations etc.

As a leader, one should be able to build a team which is based on trust and mutual respect. Trust on team spirit, individual capabilities and respect for all members. If you have developed yourself enough then you would able to give directions to people who are working with you. Their perception about you and your way of working contributes to their job satisfaction.

Most of the managers look at their own senior managers and how to satisfy them so that their career growth is ensured. This approach is not leadership but narrow individualistic focus.

You start putting different skilled people together in a project. This would be as per the requirements of what solution going to be built. Skills are easy to acquire, whereas developing right attitude takes time and effort. And as a leader it is your responsibility to give direction to your team.

Here are a few pointers towards building a team based on trust and mutual respect.

- Give respect to individual before expecting it from others. Positional leadership is valid at office. Real human connect is necessary to build a great team.

- Understand that with similar background and life experiences, everyone would behave in the same way.

- Give respect to individual knowledge and highlight their contributions explicitly, give the credit which due for them.

- Have sports and cultural activities within team it builds team naturally. Once they have connect at field, they can connect at cubicles well.

- No biased treatment for individuals. Moment you do that you lower yourself from the team point of view.

- Transparency in your communications and actions makes team follows the same.

- If you have different approaches for different people, you cannot expect collective success.

- Celebrate a day as monthly birthday where everyone's birthday falling on that month would be celebrated together.

- It is a responsibility of a manager to put team together before himself. Managers who behave they are doing a favor to team by allowing celebrations at office time, can set a wrong path.

- Leadership is best observed when you are doing your contribution and team feels they are doing it themselves.

- We are as good as our team.

- Once an individual forgoes his self- interest for sake of team interest first level of success is achieved.

Best Practices

Once we have a team in real sense; it means people are connected, respects each other and can contribute to success of a project goal along with their individual goals. Our education has taught us to be competitive and grab an opportunity. What actually needed is collaboration. This approach can give rise to ample opportunities for everyone according to their caliber. Individuals can understand this view point by taking a senior colleague in their line of operation as a mentor. Same can be applied to all hierarchies of the team.

While team is connected, spirited and ready to contribute, next level of practices can be introduced to produce enhanced results.

Some of them are listed here.

- Allocate tasks based on strengths of individuals. In a group meeting ask who wishes to take up the work which are in pipeline. When a set of people opts, choose a senior among them, to head that task/module or project. While everyone accepts, let the Senior lead have a choice to lead from back. This allows next level leader's grooming.

- Have 360 degree feedback in the team once a quarter. Let every member points out what he like and where he wants to see improvement in their leader. Enforce for every good point, there should be two improvement areas identified.

- Record those observations. Before starting similar session for same person next time, discuss the recorded points first. Let the team vouch on those points.

- Have a team meeting – Reflection – every quarter to check what they done right or wrong as team in the quarter and how to correct and where to focus on the next quarter.

- Team vison – Collect individual aspirations on what they

want to achieve during their stint in the project. Collate everyone's sentences and make a common vision, in present tense as if it is achieved. Where it sounds written as for him or her as and when one reads it.

- Mandate that vision to be read by individuals every morning and evening before leaving the work.

- Use present tense, as if it is achieved. It creates similar environment in the team when repeated daily by everyone. Over period of time one can check each person's aspirations are being met by getting such opportunity within the project. It works.

- Encourage cross skilling within the team. Allow who wants to learn on what kind of skills and from which person.

- Allow cross mentoring, team members can choose from whom they want to be mentored.

- Individual can share their work and learning during the team meeting. Both technical and managerial.

- Have face to face team meeting. Out location team can still plan to be on face to face once in a quarter wherever possible. This helps all to be on same page.

- When a person leaves the team, have a farewell event and let team share individual experience with the person as a parting gift. It not only helps to feel good but also to be ready for improvement areas.

- Have a weekly team lunch at a prescribed location. Let team connect informally once in a week.

Effectiveness at Work

We can use few simple methods which most of successful people uses to take control of their day. And get similar results to oneself. Having big picture thinking and knowing your time is limited should fuel to do best day - today.

- Begin a task with end in mind. No activities should be carried out without knowing what end result we wish to have.

- Complete what you start

- Take time to think before you leap. We get inspired momentarily and continue doing things.

- Right down your daily to do list. Early in the morning or as soon as arriving at office. Having list gives a sense of direction. It does not matter how much of it completed or not.

- Set a deadline for activities.

- Have public deadline within the team. It makes people accountable.

- Right dressing. Perceptions through eyes are instantaneous. Being professionally dressed gives a sense of seriousness and responsibility. It affects both the wearer and the people who interacts with him or her.

- Display energy and smile. Your presence should add energy to the room. Develop that kind of personality

- Conference call can be used for communicating message. Seeing the messenger makes great difference.

Right G & O

Goals and objectives are defined for an appraisal year. It will have all the details which are expected to be achieved for a role in that year. A rough guideline. Corporates have roles and G & O mapping done as templates. It serves the overall expectations. Coming to individuals, it can be tailor made on what kind of work one wishes to do. Also get him to evaluate on the works he is actually doing.

While templates help, realistic G & O is responsibility of both individual and the manager. Take time to arrive at the tailor made objectives for entire team. Let team know what are the objectives from the junior most to the manager and above. Make them available to be referred anytime. Team can use that to consider their growth plan.

Constantly think, why I am on payroll, what is expected out of my contribution, what is my career road map for next 2 – 3 years and what are my highest value activities. These question should be addressed by ones G & O. Too many objectives can diluting the focus. Have maximum of 5 distinct areas. Know which one to take up as priority, quarter wise.

Maintain monthly folder in your system to track your contributions made by you. Have your G & O pasted at your work area and encourage your team to do so.

With right G & O you know where you are positioned with respect to contributions you have made. You would genuinely know your year-end ratings yourself. You don't need your supervisor rating to tell what you have done is good or not so good. It prevents you don't fall prey to blame game.

A belief that your supervisor can take care you may be detrimental in terms of real growth as professional. while it may be true for brief a period of time.

Steve Young puts it very well, *'the principle is competing against yourself. It's about self-improvement, about being better than you were the day before'.*

Gen Y

Gen Y is excited about life. When their excitement and energy made turn inwards, it can serve to expect more, from themselves.

Exciting work life, fun filled, adventurous, glittering and dark colors attracts their attention easily. It includes free food and frequent parties.

On the other side of Gen-Y, some may lack patience, have scattered ideas, inability to focus for long time, enjoy what is easier to learn, all these are normal. Their preference includes travel, do work as if it is a hobby, more leaves, resist close supervision and walk away style are also common.

Most wish to be busy with activities, rather spending time on planning or to know the big picture. They like competitions, prizes and recognitions.

Getting their view point, giving them attention for the their creativity and allowing them to choose their work items wherever possible, helps to gain their confidence on your part as manager.

Through the media, they have access to see the world class business leaders and their style, approach and knowledge. So it becomes natural to look to such role model in their reach at work place. Once you as a manger prove that you have similar qualities of world class leaders, then you become their role model.

A team with confidence on their leader and on his or her steering abilities will boost team morale. Directly helps to achieve more in short span of time.

Management Vs Leadership

Let the team debate on this topic once in quarter. It develops a deeper understanding on, what are the qualities of a good manager and of a leader. With repeated debates, team develops clarity where they are heading as individuals. It practically aids people to develop on leadership.

When they see a not so good practices of others, they can develop ability to voice their view with right sense of judgment. This help teams to become better leaders for tomorrow.

Take few popular HBR business cases for group debate within the team. Ask their views to segregate as managers' approach and what would be the leaders approach. Develop their ability to think and voice their views within the team comfortably. Here every one is given equal opportunity to showcase their thinking and to learn to value others point of view.

You may note some of these points in the discussions.

Managers	Leaders
Talks about tasks and results	Talks about vision & possibilities
Believes in success formulae	Innovates new ways
Stepwise improvement	Paradigm shift
Avoids risks	Understand risk and rewards
Showcases green status as late as possible	Keen on Identifying red early for course correction
Managers drive business	Leaders develop people

Charismatic leadership possible in most of the circumstances. Leadership does not come with position, but with self, the individual. Position can aid to enhance leadership, if it is already present in a person. Otherwise easy way is to get aligned with a better leader and learn firsthand.

Evidences of a Good Team

You can take a stroll within the work place of your team and try to figure out what is their state of mind. Here are a few observations.

- If they are happy, they greet you with natural welcoming smile, wish to shake hands with you and asks without inhibitions your personal things or comment on your dressing. It shows they are connected with you and your leadership is evident.

- Weekend shifts, holiday shifts will be volunteered by the team, not because of the extra wages, but because individuals want to prove themselves on extra miles.

- People spend at others desk to help on a problem he or she is facing. You may find more than 2- 3 people try to help on that work .

- You often see people go to lunch and tea breaks together

- There may be smaller celebration within the team for birthday, anniversary, child birth etc.

- People volunteer to visit on colleagues hospitalization or one of their family members.

On the other hand if they try to stick to their desktop, pretend to be working on serious issue, give you short answers, avoid natural eye contact for long then you know your effectiveness is that of a manager.

|7|

FINANCIAL FREEDOM

A man in debt is like an empty bag; neither of them can sit upright - unknown

Why Freedom

Why discussion on financial freedom in a book on career, we will soon understand by going through this chapter.

As one develops towards leadership, I have observed lot of people don't show up because of the feeling they carry towards job security. With false thinking of job security they forgo the financial security. Which one can earn themselves if they employ their time and efforts in the right direction. A job is a temporary solution for a longer range problem.

Any limiting belief should be overcome as we move towards authentic leadership. Having sufficient financial resources at our disposal and self-restrained life style can give tremendous scope towards individual's growth.

Being financially free makes us fit to be undisturbed from money and career pressure. It makes us start working towards our real passion and start thinking about contribution to society with the skills acquired. Once the financial goals are met we will have ample time to focus on our non-financial goals in life.

Hence this chapter proves important.

Without being free from if's and buts of life, we are not able to express ourselves freely . A sense of freedom from money thinking has to be developed consciously. As long as we see money as a mode of fulfilling our needs, then we master it. Needs vary according to lifestyle of individuals. As we grow in career, we need to know how to employ money in right ways, so that it works for us. While we work towards our passion.

I have observed that while our career gives a lot opportunities to learn and grow, it is actually at the expense of our time. Moreover, it does not guarantee that one can become rich. Answer lies in financial education. Financial education has to be pursued by individual, since it is not taught in our academic syllabus.

When we become financially independent our progress in the outer world skyrockets. We will not hesitate sharing what is right. Nor we depend on somebody's opinion about us. We carry higher self-respect and self-worth in our eyes and that reflects in our voice, tone, walk and even in the way we look at things.

This can happen when we make money in right way. Otherwise same money can make us behave timid, double minded or double faced. How we earn our money matters most. A financially free person will be able to understand how this world functions holistically and to lead a unperturbed life. Which is worth striving for.

Start Early

This is the basic mantra for financial freedom. In that process, we are tapping time value of the money. Financial education can start as early as in teen age. Since it is a matter of commonsense, it should start at least with your first salary.

I have come across people who simply followed a single step to freedom by saving 25% of their earnings every month. And put them in PPF or EPF. Over a 12 – 15 years, this single investment could generate passive income enough to take care of their fixed expenditures. Similar results can come to people investing maximum amount in tax saving instruments every fiscal year.

Authentic learning is having a clear picture of where we are now and to know how our future should look like. If we understand any philosophy first then it is easier to accommodate the learning in a holistic way.

While individual thinks job is the only way of making money, then that job itself can come in the way of becoming rich. Last few years of your career has filled up, more of your financial needs. As one grow in the career ladder, it is natural life style also grows. In fact, it has now put you up with a situation paying of EMI every month. For the car you own or for the house and for the luxuries you hardly have time to use it. Invariably making us continue to hold on to the job.

When we are in debt half of our creativity dies. We are simply not able to think clearly. If we can disconnect ourselves from money sense or career sense our progress as individual towards leadership can fasten. Most often people does not give a thinking about financial freedom much specially in professional circles.

Financial freedom gives ability to deal with multiple options. In the situation of lack of financial resources, you have a choice imposed on you. To break this barrier, we need to be financially educated. This is possible and practical. Once you learnt different ways of earning your passive income, you can jump start working on your passion which can lead you to be unique in your area of interest.

Early start prevents regretting later years.

Our Excuses

We often hear people saying why they are poor. Some of them can be: we are not in business; our parents were not rich; being rich is not for everyone; money is bad; it requires money to make money; I should have born 10 years earlier and many more.

A simple arithmetic. Check on how much you have earned by way of your of salary or income vs. how much money has earned for you.

Money works for you by the way of appreciating its value while invested rightly in real estate, fixed deposits and commodities. Making money work for you will liberate, while you working for money leads to slavery. This has to be understood clearly and emphatically.

When money is employed rightly it generates income which we call as passive income. Income where we don't employ our time to earn it. In other words we work once and money keeps coming multiple times. Examples like rentals, royalties or franchise fees.

While we are on job, we are doing *addition*, we are paid hourly basis and we earn as much hours as we put into the work. There can be a limit. 8 hours a day. Financial freedom sense comes from the fact that, if you learn how to multiply our 8 hours, through entrepreneur mind set we achieve *multiplication*. Then we can earn more in same number of hours.

360 Degree Financial Planning

Basic financial freedom lies in taking measures against the known or possible expenditure when it comes. Have a steady plan of saving or investing towards that purpose. Idea here is to take care of every known major expenses. so that nothing in life comes as surprise and takes away our savings.

Here are few areas everyone needs to look at first.

- Life insurance
- Medical insurance
- Retirement planning
- Tax planning
- Education, marriage (self & children)
- Vehicle
- Housing
- Foreign vacation
- Any other hazards insurances.

While your monthly income first takes care of these basic expenditures, then it gives you a tremendous sense of freedom from unknowns. Your mind will be now free to be more creative and can help plan early retirement that you dream of. You may add any more purposes you have in life which needs financial inputs.

Also you should start learning not to simply accumulate things or wealth, without having its end use in mind. I have seen over period of time managing the accumulated wealth itself can take ones precious time, which one may wish to employ elsewhere.

Beauty is when we do financial planning religiously our mind becomes free from if's and but's of life so that one can completely focus on the most important thing, working towards our passion.

A Good Debt

Since you have a steady pay slip, it helps to raise the capital for your investments easily. Lot of the financial institutes will be willing to lend you money as loan. Utilize every opportunity in doing so.

We talked about doing MBA while you are on payroll. If you are doing so with an educational loan you can get tax exemption on the interest you pay. Similar to a housing loan.

People may have hesitation in opting for a loan. Because of the responsibility involved in its repayments. This is an excuse. Real problem is our risk taking ability. Like our body muscles which can be developed with right work outs and food habits; financial mind can be developed by taking risks.

Calculated risks can be taken by anyone. Risk is something where outcome is uncertain. You take measures to increase the possibility of odds in your favor.

Know yourself better. Go through multiple 'Risk Analyzers' in the internet. They can give you a fair idea of what is your risk taking ability. Once you understand that well, then next step is slowly moving out of your comfort zone by practice. With risk taking ability the possibilities of raising capital comes easily; you can tap time value of money through wise investments. With right vision and periodically tracking your investments can generate ample returns over a period of time. You may use capital to develop money generating assets. Good debt is one which actually grows beyond the cost of money acquired.

I have observed people can achieve their financial freedom in 3 to 5 years if they are really devoted to the subject. I have listed few of them here in this book which are extract from the sessions I conduct on financial freedom.

A Business of Investing

Since you are a professional and focusing more to do on career front, ideal ways for multiple income would be those areas where you don't have to be physically present to do things.

Being an investor helps here. Looking at trading possibilities, stock trading or investment in real estate, chit funds, P2P lending all can come handy.

Start with trading of your two wheeler, four wheeler or even real estate. Money in motion produces more and you learn art of dealing and negotiating with people. This is essential as we do bigger business deals later in life.

I have witnessed many millionaires who are comfortable in accumulating money. There are not willing to dispose some of their assets and produce liquidity to improve their life style. That can be a trap. Attachment towards anything helps increasing misery not growth.

If our wealth does not help towards educating ourselves further, for higher possibilities, then we are forgetting the basic rule of leveraging on our strengths. Otherwise we may end up becoming millionaires but actually not being free. It is a trap many suffer.

I advocate serious efforts on learning towards disconnecting with our accumulations and continue focusing on massive returns and systemize the entire process. This way we will have ample time and money to do most important things in life, self-development and contribution to society. People start seeking a role model in you.

Develop the mind set of trusteeship, towards anything you own. You learn the way of making money and not get struck with what you have; it will prove as a royal road to become a person of truly free in nature.

I have noted, money itself does not make any person good or bad. It only enhances what he or she already is.

Rich and not so rich

It is important to understand the difference. We are traversing on the path which leads to richness both in mind and material. Understanding these differences will helps to achieve it faster. Moreover it can help us to understand why are we not rich yet. If anyone has done it before then it should encourage us to do it that way.

Take time to study the rich people around you or those you see on screen, when you look closely at their habits and thinking, you start finding what is missing in you. Most of the time it may appear to be a particular skill, but beneath it you will find it is actually the mindset and not the money or skills.

Here are few pointers from the book *secrets of millionaire mindset,* which can make one think in that direction.

- Rich are aware, others not awake
- Rich plan early, others reacts late
- Rich works smart, other works hard
- Rich risks, other avoids best mitigated risks
- Rich adapts, others avoids
- Rich enjoys, others exists
- Rich improves constantly, others stagnates
- Rich respects money, others says money is so not important
- Rich sells themselves, others hides
- Rich encourages, others envies

Developing a spirit of collaboration fastens the road to richness. There is no fun becoming richer alone. Join a master mind group where members work on investments avenues and helps to grow each other.

Arrive at right corpus

Lots of time we are under the illusion that we need lots of money before we can start work on our passion undisturbed. Practicality may be different. By the time we finish with the accumulating money through *addition* we would have exhausted our energy, physical and mental or both.

I found it is always better to start small with where we are and with what we have. It helps to check whether such a passion is real or it's a mere excuse to escape from the reality. When we start doing instead of dreaming we are bound to test our suitability. Both ourselves and to the nature of activities. So that if it does not suit we can move on without losing much money or time. Test each passion in a similar way, until we find out the one which works for us.

A real passion, you find it energizes you on the move.

Basic financial freedom is to maintain the life style we are familiar with; without having to work for money. This way we would stay comfortable and be able to think naturally. Most of the time even lowering life style can achieve the financial freedom faster. It is again individual choice.

Alternatively follow the rule to identify your freedom figure.

Fixed expenditures amount per month	- X
Variable expenditures for a month	- Y
Total expenditures = X+Y	= Z

For a year it would be Z X 12 Months   = XYZ Amount.

Once we have XYZ every year available to us via different means apart from salary income, we are financially free. Next idea should be how to generate this XYZ amount every year through passive way. In a nutshell that is our work for financial freedom. For simplicity, omitting taxation, inflation and exigencies part in the above calculation.

A simple bank interest of 5% a year can produce XYZ amount then what would be the corpus we needed for that. That is our freedom corpus. ABC X 5/100 = XYZ

Here after our primary aim would be to accumulate corpus ABC amount. So that our yearly expense of XYZ is taken care. Interest rate / return varies based on the kind of investment you make. This entirely follows risk and reward correlations.

Freedom Formulae

Below formulae summarize the endeavors required in order to achieve the financial freedom. There may be a better alternative to it through inheritance or marriage.

However a person who does not know the *money language* will not be able to hold his fortunes for long time or get benefit out of it. We have seen examples of sudden richness via lottery, insurance, which later follows coming back to original state or similar pattern, across the world .

Financial Freedom =

Multiple Income Sources + Saving & Investment + Passive Income + Lifestyle simplification + Financial Education

- Multiple income source – Salary is one source of income + income from business or agriculture
- Savings – it is that amount you take out from your income first before every other expenditure. Not what is left over end of the month.

- Investments – which produces income in the form of dividends, interests etc.

- Passive income – rentals, royalties, franchise fee

- Lifestyle simplification – reduce unnecessary purchases and accumulation

- Financial Education – constantly get educated for growth as individual and keep up with the financial world. It helps to grow further with what we already have.

A PERSONAL LIFE STAGE

This section describes your personal life while you are carried with your middle management career.

You have been married and with family and having children. A good project manager also need to be good in life management.

You will learn to organize things at personal front, which includes money matters and keeping yourself clear mind and stress less.

Most of parents try to put their dreams on children. And hope they would able to carry on with the desires which, as parents they could not make at it. They push children towards their dreams. This can create a stressful situation for everyone involved.

Sooner we will find out our children learn from our behaviors not from what we teach. So being an ideal parent while kids are smaller, is easier. As they grow they start comparing with the parents of their friends. By the time they reach teens they would start comparing you with the role models they see in the media.

It is wise to become a role models to your children. So they continue to respect you as they grow. They try to model your life. For this staying relevant and updating with latest developments in the world becomes necessary.

Necessity of learning does not stop throughout one's life.

ACTION EXERCISE

A Typical Day

- You have established with your daily dozen. Those practices which keep your energy up all day long.

- These includes exercise, meditation or power nap to recharge yourself for remaining half of the day and many more.

- To do more in less time means one need to be physically fit and mentally alert. Business of money loves speed.

- You now understand the meaning between the lines, those on the lines and communication through silence.

- As a good manager of yourself, you would keep your energy level up with proper food rest and focus.

Learning Areas

- Read two books in a month. Now skimming through the popular best seller will help. Where there is a point you can make use of it for your practice on fields.

- Making time for attending children's school related works

- You learnt it is no more time management it is energy management.

- You have learnt the importance of financial freedom to enjoy the life ahead.

- If we are not careful, we have lots of money but no energy left to utilize that in right direction.

- You also notice cases where children from deprived class of society are doing better at school, because they have thirst for achievements.

Recommendations

- Seven habits of highly effective people – Stephen Covey
- Goals – Brian Tracy
- Magic of Big thinking – David J. Schwartz
- Lazy Project manager – Peter Taylor
- Cash flow Quadrant – Robert Kiyosaki
- Secrets of Millionaire Mindset – Harv T Eker
- Millionaire Next Door - Thomas J. Stanley
- Men are from Mars and Women are from Venus – John Grey
- www.mindtools.com

PART IV

SENIOR MANAGEMENT

NAVEEN CHANDRA

FOCUS AREA

This section discusses about the skills and mindset required at senior management level. Typical age will be 40 years and above.

You have travelled far in your career and life. You have learnt by experience what works with you, because you have observed the pattern repeatedly.

You may wish to take career further in the corporate ladder and move into strategic planning team, CXO level positions if that thrills you still. Nothing wrong.

As progress in corporate happens you find it is pyramid shaped. Only few positions are there in the top floor, while shop floor can accommodate more because mostly it is a skill based repetitive works.

At senior management one is expected to be best of the breed. He should be able to sense where the industry is heading towards and know how to align to get the first mover advantage. Decisions here, can make or break the resources accumulated.

If you can define where industry moves or even give direction, then you are an exceptional business leader that makes you high in demand among the peer circles. You would be treated as an industry expert.

Lot of people deviate here because they understand what they really want in life and what can provide lasting satisfaction for having lead life fully.

This section focuses on both the aspects. Giving a gist of the skills needed here, having edge with technical, people and entrepreneur ship mindset and as well as on mindset shift required as great giver to the society.

Let's go through the ideas here.

|8|

THE BIG PICTURE

At the age of fifty I knew where is my destiny
– Confucius.

Think BIG

Big picture thinking is about having all the aspects taken care including business, region, legal advantages and people or even more. Over period of time one find it becomes natural thinking, but to begin with we may have to consciously cultivate it.

People start thinking to get the best out of the investment and from the business ideas. To suite such thinking one may look out for the opportunities available in his or her interest's direction in terms of supporting government policies, exchange advantage, labor costs and many more things.

This is essential to lead from the strategic point of view. Because you are setting up a big enterprise or new business idea on a platform which is set for success. Taking advantage of inner circle people, reputation you carry within the industry and in public domain helps a lot to get right investors contacts.

Your innovative ideas, creativeness is definitely an USP you carry along with your entrepreneur mind set. Whether its running a role in corporate or being on your own. It matters.

A Shared Vision

While arriving at business model, what matters most is the right team. Who have completely understand each other's interests and strengths.

This initial founder team understanding only can make the flight stronger. Making a business plan with a horizon of 3 – 5 years view is a must. Ability to arrive at and review each aspect of the business is very crucial. Lot of time should be spent on brain storming, getting expert opinions, arriving at a shared vision where everyone feels connected is most important.

If team is not connected, then individuals interest becomes paramount over the vison. We can see when individuals interest is more than the vision of the company, then the entire business case is a failure, however well it is articulated.

It is always vision which keeps people together. It enables new talents who aspires to be a part of such vision possible. Vision of making money is a poor vision. Money should be an outcome of adding value to the customers. So that team strives for customer satisfaction while money part is taken care in itself.

If any of the founder member not aligned to the core value and vision of the company still he or she can be used as consultant because of his or her skills for a certain period of time. Keeping individual interests above the vision of the organization usually ends with short growth.

Good thing I have observed in a shared goal is, when one of the stakeholders takes time away for any personal reasons, venture can still continue without much disturbances. Whereas if there is no shared goal, people are bound to wait for orders and they don't tend to be proactive by nature.

Merger, Acquisition and Joint Venture

Business can take up a shape through acquisition of an existing business entity. Through this channel there is already a promised business and activities in pipeline. Enterprises prefer this way of growth since it just adds the missing link and expands the business, which the organization is already into.

May be with a particular technology partner, a partner in the particular geographical area, where company B has a good hold. It works as an easier way for marketing the added service lines. And to start offering the new services to existing customers without much of the gestation period.

Skills required on the technical front, business decision, skills in hiring right team and skills in negotiation all matter here most.

Competitive spirit helps only for a certain period. If competition continues longer run, each business tries to come out with more features for their product there by making it better than the other one available.

Over a period of time the base cost of the product rises high due to add-ons. These add-ons may not be used or required in most of the cases for end users.

The spirit of collaboration takes away the unnecessary items in both the partners. It identifies and equates what is good in each other and finally enhances the joint product at a lesser cost. This kind of JV's will be useful for all the stake holders.

This requires leader mind set to operate from and not from that of scarcity.

Fund Raising

Raising funds for new business or initiative within your corporate can be challenging. Convincing, vision and revenue generation can be an exercise very few would enjoy doing.

The point to be noted here is, there is no way money can come to you unless you have a backup of your past success and you are an industry figure. For the rest of us we have to go through a set of procedures to prove our business intent and our roadmap are flawless.

All best planned businesses will have unknown challenges. While execution has to be taken care boldly, but inability to spend enough time to make an idea as a concrete business case cannot be excused. All such initiatives which are done in hurry to prove something, usually do not see a life more than 1 to 2 years.

People don't pump money on business which is only consuming. Big plans can take years of preparation, if that is the part of the plan then it is acceptable. Once the business has started then any delay in putting up the complete circle can be a very costly, because it affects. Revenue generation should happen at earliest.

Most of the entrepreneurs fail here because they don't plans to have intermediate revenue generation areas. They wait till the entire product is ready. Then continue improving that product while their investments goes only as inputs to the business. This model may not sustain long run. This is similar to eating away the golden goose, whereas what is desired is to work with its golden eggs.

Both innovation and revenue generation should happen together and in parallel to sustain the basic cost of the businesses involved.

Angel Investor and Venture Capital

Entrepreneurship is an act of courage. You are putting your dreams into reality. It can be very inspiring, exciting, tiresome and rewarding, depending on what stage of the business you are in. Most of the startup requires more energy, more hurdles to face and consumes more time and money than expected. One has to be prepared in that direction too.

There are cash rich individuals who look for right people and business ideas where they can take a calculated risk on their investments. They would involve in the management of the business with the interest as an investor. Every investor would enter a business with a clean exit plan defined.

This model can also come as a venture capital funding with same set of interests and trust in your business ideas.

There are incubation centers which promotes new business ideas aligning to particular set of industry segments.

Banks give funding based on your project and collaterals you can offer. Government schemes, SEZ promotions all are useful, VC funding. But none will work the way you have imagined. So be prepared to move from failure to failure. Then the entrepreneurship is suitable for you and also the grand success it can offer.

Funds may also be raised through own savings, friends, relatives and from high net worth individuals. Most of the time this helps you to realize who are your true friends. I call this as Test of Money. It never fails to reveal the nature of a person and never lies.

It always reveals the leadership beneath.

Initial Public Offer

Once you have made your brand in industry and have multiple customers across different locations and your business repute is good, then you can go for raising public money via initial public offer.

You highlight your past performances and future plans. Highlight where and how money being raised would be used for. What would be the likely dividend you can offer as part of a profitable business.

You had been investing in stock market as part of financial education and freedom. Now it is time to come up with your own firm share and list them in popular stock exchanges based on your location of business. If you are not keen enough to go public, you can go through private placements owning a private company.

Raising funds can be cumbersome effort if you have not already proved your worth in the industry circles.. Here Murphy's law becomes evident. *'Anything which can go wrong, will go wrong'*

When you look from the perspective of a business man, then you see a different picture, the work which was exciting to you as an employee now it has to become like place of worship!. You need to have same devotion to make it a successful enterprise. 24/7 is less until you systemize the business. Thinking as systems is not easier task for many entrepreneurs. It is quite easy for a person who comes from corporate background. You have witnessed efficient systems functioning with multiple customers.

Rich Dad definition of business comes handy here. A good business would grow, even if you are on vacation for a year. This is possible only when you have policy, procedure, templates, checklists, and all other things which you have learned in the 'process orientation'.

While it is not easier to appreciate the focus on the process being busy with sales and marketing functions, the bread winner for enterprise. Yet importance of high quality norms should be introduced in the beginning of the business itself.

Top and Bottom lines

Basic belief required for any entrepreneur is that, *I am in the best business*. For success of business as unit in a corporate or even a business owned by you, sooner you identify there should be a constant flow of new business revenues. Repeat business revenues helps to keep the smooth flowing of an organization.

Revenue from new products, markets etc., add to top line. The process efficiency, right usage of the production facilities, handling employees or machineries backup can help optimize the cost involved in the production, the bottom line.

A constant watch on both these parameters are crucial. Most of the entrepreneurs are busy targeting the top line and forget there can be a better way of doing everything. Optimizing the cost of production can be a source for constant improvement.

Soon one will realize business is all about relationships. Your customer comes to you not because of not only the product but who you are as a person and why you're doing the business. Keeping yourself humble, up to date on the industry and being approachable helps to retain the existing customers. And to grow from the references of those who you serve. Because they have first-hand experience of your offerings.

Being humble, developing personal connect does not only mean you go out of the way to make people happy about your services. It is also about how you do that and how your people do it as part of policy.

Do you consider your customer success as primary
Do you meet your key customers every quarter
Do you study where other areas of customer you can serve
Do you recommend a better service to customer and where to get it from.

You understand how reputation as an individual, as a big brand have effect on the consumer world. People see you as a special person with lot of knowledge and how you have put that in the welfare of a society.

Turning as Investor

While building a business excites you means developing a brand, developing people you consider as assets also encourage you. Soon you will find a better way of doing it. It is time to become an investor.

You can identify a potential person to develop the business under your guidance and produce more of similar businesses at the same time. Your effectiveness as investor can be huge. A leader always develops more leaders. It will become a good gauge of success as a leader. Because you know your time is limited and you wish to make best out of it for yourself and for others.

Incubation centers. They are set up for two reasons. One to encourage the entrepreneurs and another to catch hold of the upcoming business models right at its infancy so as get the first mover advantage to your fold. You may generally start with in house incubation center or VC funding allocated in the corporate sector.

Your repute as an expert in the industry or business world gives you enough exposure to seek the investment opportunities. Though it would be difficult to find and promote a good business; but at level of maturity you have attained by now, it should a possible and an enjoyable journey itself. Moreover it makes you a proud of giving your knowledge to right mentees as well.

I have come across a few multimillionaires, who are just looking for people with right mindset. Then they part their knowledge gained without any hesitation or expectation. Because they feel that is the right thing to do from their side.

When you are not ready to take up the responsibilities as an investor you can stay as a mentor or management consultant working for the growth of others businesses and help boost their leadership capabilities.

A Social Enterprise

Concept of social entrepreneurship is becoming more these days. It comes with a focused group of people addressing a business need. With professionally managed structure taking up a social cause as the main reason to do business. They start with self-sufficiency mode and they move to profit making for re-investing back into the business expansion or refining their product range.

A good leader can get attention of many likeminded fellows in a community or region. Since he or she is a known public figure, people who have developed respect for the individual or his business concepts would be the investors or the first level team.

It usually begins with a set of volunteers who have significant experiences in that area. As well necessary business skills with service oriented approach towards it.

These social enterprises can do a huge impact, since people there are working for a cause other than the profit alone as compared to regular commercial enterprises. Here development of people, enhancing their living standards, providing a model with buy back arrangement of the produces are the main focus.

FPO's can be similar entities supported by flexible terms by government itself. When people have done their best in corporate world, then look at giving back to society as social enterprises. Since they know the dynamics required to run a huge enterprise. If they prefer to be mentors and supporter of individuals having clear conscience, their experience and wealth can be put in right usage.

Having a foundation, charity, NGO are some of the popular ways of giving back to society.

NAVEEN CHANDRA

| 9 |

LIVING THE LEGACY

Always be ready to speak your mind and a base man will avoid you. — William Blake

A Legend

If you have come to this chapter and think this is too much to strive for. Yes it is. Living a life of achievement, contribution and fulfilment takes time and ardent efforts. If it is easier then every one of us would have achieved it. Everyone is capable, provided we have taken time to correct, refocus and develop ourselves on the move.

Leadership development can start with our ability to accept when we are wrong. A journey of leadership never ends, because you see lessons will always come to refine you from different corners. What is important, is that journey already has started?

While you grow from campus to corporate, the journey depicted here may sounds easy and simple. Answer is YES only because you had a right mindset coupled with dedicated, focused efforts and willing to correct yourself. It puts you across an edge over others.

Otherwise answer is NO.

Challenges, everyone faces on the path of growth. There is nothing waiting out there for you to go and play around. One has to create his or her playground, know every rule how the game is played, so that you don't go out of the game anytime sooner.

Take time to learn the game in the right way and play with heart out. Know that either one can win or lose, because it is a game. Any attachment to the particular outcome can make one suffer.

An attitude of being humble and ready to learn from people who have done it better, should always exist. Irrespective of how much we have grown and wherever we are in the journey. And you have to decide your playground. Is that at corporate?, at your state or country or beyond. No body sets that limit, it is set inside one's mind.

With all these progress, one still has to take up the challenges which lays ahead. Once you win the battle you have enough time to relax and ponder. If one avoids the battle he or she will never be able to develop as a finest human being.

I remember what Raymond Smith, former CEO of Bell Atlantic Corporation once remarked, *'Administrators are easy to find and cheap to keep. Leaders – risk takers- are in very short supply. And ones with vision are pure gold'*

Making of a leader

Everybody is a leader. As leaders we have to share a collective vision and be bold enough to let the team know what they can be. The results will astonish us far beyond our own expectations.

We have learnt leadership is not about position or a fancy title. It is an attitude any one can take up towards his life. It is about the ability to give direction and able to make contribution towards the growth of the fellow beings. Be it in the team, business or social circle. Leadership evolves when one is out of the temptation of money, position or popularity or any other.

Leadership development takes time and effort. There have been different approaches, suggestions, experiments and polls on what is relevant and effective. What I have learnt is, there no one size fitting for all kind solution out there. As leader one should be adaptable to pick the relevant style suitable to different categories of problem or people or situation involved.

The journey is making a sculpture out of one's raw form and then presenting to the world in a manner which is acceptable and also adorable.

At this stage life has given you good and bad experiences to arrive at a personal philosophy which actually suits to your individuality . Ideally one would be looking at contribution to society with whatever has been experienced and learnt.

Interestingly one can reach to leadership level without climbing the corporate ladder, however the nature of challenges would remain more are less same.

Satisfaction of having lived life comes from putting our best every day, in right direction. 80:20 rule applies here. Most of us are settled for life of ordinary.

Living the Legacy

Great, you have made it to world class.

You are now bold enough, that, hesitation, fearful nature of yours has gone away. It is replaced with confident and realistic based thinking. This approach gives you a tremendous satisfaction.

If you observe your financial freedom gives you the base on which you can operate on leadership without compromising the lifestyle and values you have developed.

Many a times when the designation is removed from life, then there is vacuum; nothing to attach and individuals feel blank suddenly. This may happen in any part of life if we are attached to anything of materialistic value. Getting trapped in any area of life for long can be a problem.

Once you have satisfied yourself with kind of sculpting you have done to your life, that is consciously designing your life. It is now time to share those knowledge, those accumulations. So a sense of being useful to society becomes prominent. Here comes leaving the legacy.

I prefer living the legacy. Who knows what is there is store when we all become dust. Leaving the legacy may be easier, who would be there to know it. So start living the legacy based on your experiences and knowledge. As long as those things are in use, you are living your legacy, whether your mortality exists or not it should not matter much.

Run your own race

While you sit calmly and see back the journey of making yourself as a leader, kind of risks you have taken, situations you have faced, right decisions taken irrespective of the gains or losses all have contributed to your growth.

You understand becoming a millionaire, a corporate leader or business tycoon, all is a game of making yourself a better human. Getting best of life is more important than getting best of our career.

It is time to decide the priorities again. When you start searching for an answer you find there are not many people around for help. You start getting hints that if nature has given more to you, then it is expecting more from you. It is a time to believe oneself in becoming an instrument in the hands of nature.

You realize the ways of self-development has taken you beyond average human capacity. Thinking smaller goals is smaller for you now, because of your capacity to do more. Ability to see good in everything slowly develops as ability to do good for all. Win-Win or no deal as suggested by Stephen covey.

You are a leader now that you have aspired to become once. You have learnt the principles which are needed. After years of development you will come to a stage when you understand that there is joy in giving service. Working for a cause is more important than any other things. In such pursuit you look for people with right mind set, who can be evolved to next level.

All the experience we have undergone is for developing more leaders for future. And if our knowledge, experience and learning do not make us better persons, more loving and more fulfilling in life then what is the point of having them all in first place ?.

Understand that anything can come to us only when we are open enough. It is always a collaborative effort from nature to work through individual consciousness to express its ideas and flavors. One can work as extended arm of it, doing our best, putting the shared vision ahead and oneself below it.

Honestly, it is what we seek we get, if we seek less, we get less.

Who am I

You are what you do repeatedly, however nice we may portray. Actions speak louder than words.

Identifying who we are rightly allows to win the battle more than 50% of the time. We have multiple tastes, interests and passions. To be at the pinnacle of leadership, we need to be ready to give up the good we have accumulated in order to get the best waiting for us. Our inability to give up things which we have, blocks what can come into our life. Fear of losing what we have becomes stronger over period of time. It was easier to give up in earlier stages of the career and life. Because stakes were less.

You now know, you can make it to any level of success. It depends on multiple factors and you know which one to choose and when. Questions like -

Is this right way ?
Is this what I have to do ?
Does this still excites me as much as it used to be ?

Some where you feel you are here to contribute more than earning lots of money.

What should I do

This is the important question to be asked based on the enormous experience of life is at stake. I have observed, in the matter of making anything, there is no end. People pursue some or other thing to get a sense of achievement.

I found good way for a leader is to start giving away what has been accumulated over years. This ensures two things, knowing our mortality and ensuring the next generation benefits from the gist of experience sharing.

- Look at social enterprise possibilities
- Develop the area of society which concern you most
- Develop leadership academy around your learnings
- Write a book
- Educate people
- Sponsor hospitals
- Animal welfare
- Any idea which touches your heart

Whatever you would do at this level, it would be unique and fulfilling. You would not spend any time in beating around the bush but only focus on how much you can give away and how quickly it is possible.

Since you have the social connect at similar peer groups with more or less similar ideas, you find it is easier to implement your ideas or support their ideas which is based on benefiting large number of people.

No excuse at Death

However we claim on our knowledge and ability to do good to the fellow beings, our inner conscience always points out the better way of doing it.

It's true, with repeated negative approaches one takes can silence the voice of conscience during the hay time. Same voice gains its control back once the person mellows down with the biological aging. While we are not able exert our full potential in the conscious way, voice may haunt us back in later days.

Sounds much philosophical ?, Every leader would know that what he could have done better; had he given up certain thinking, certain mental blocks, certain perceptions and expectations. We feel true freedom when we stop expecting from the fellow beings and start expecting more from ourselves.

A feeling of having done our best with the time, skills and opportunities provided to us. Having the satisfaction in the contributions made to the world in making it a better place for living, should be aimed at.

As a leader we have been given the knowledge, training and opportunity to do it at the top, to set expectations, to guide people and give the direction with the best of our knowledge and abilities.

If we have not done that as part of our leadership there is something amiss, the essence of humanity.

End matters the most.

Leaders grow leaders

Once the essence of leadership is experienced firsthand and have gained the confidence in executing many projects, programs simultaneously, one may start looking at developing the right leaders to follow the roadmap.

Developing leadership skills while working with leader is easier. Otherwise it requires enormous amount of courage and belief in oneself. To put his ideas in front of his team, learn from failure, correct self-mistakes and giving away the glory to others. This is how ground level leadership would start.

Harold Geneen once said *'Leadership cannot really be taught. It can only be learnt'*. Very opt.

When a person gets right stage to execute an idea or have lineage it may be easier to go ahead. Individual who aspire to develop on leadership have to undergo many trials to hone his or her leadership skills. It easier when everything is green. Real leadership will be known at the time of crisis. It reveals who we really are, however nice we might think of ourselves.

Learn to leave every interaction as if it is the last one. It helps to be at our best, more courteous in our behaviors. And who knows it can be the last one too. Don't let yourself to take anything granted.

This approach helps ourselves to be cautious and know that resources which we may have now, should be used properly to enhance it. Person who knows his energy and skills are limited by time, would be able to contribute more to society in a hurried manner.

The 21st Century Leadership

In 21st century leadership there is one common striking point, it's a leadership of collective vision. People wish to be the part of a growth plan, to have a sense of belongingness as a person and attempt to make the world a better place to live and love. And it is becoming a norm.

More social enterprises, partner with government in their endeavors, collaborations are doing better work. It is a platform where individuality, creativity and a mode to express themselves fully. This allow collective positivity to be flown in the right direction based on the leader's experience.

It requires a charismatic, friendly, competent, knowledgeable leader to be among the Gen Y; who are looking forward for a direction. This is a time where so much of confusions due to multiples options available at ease. In my interactions, I have found there are lot more Gen Y who are looking right role models among their reach whom they can aspire to follow.

We talked about strengths of Gen Y, whose buying tastes are defining the business and economic growth all over the globe. Charismatic leadership work better with them, because of the energy they carry, the sportive spirit they have and the power of social media recognitions. Moreover they would have witnessed the leaders across the globe.

A leader who can tap this force by providing a right reason, vision and alignment can achieve superior results in a short span of time. If organizations can create such leaders, a lot more dynamism can be brought into day to day work life.

21st Century Leadership requires a connect at heart, ability to look at each other's eyes and in having a collective vision.
Results will astonish far beyond expectations; a positive work environment, talent retention, business growth and customer's delight.

A PERSONAL LIFE STAGE

This section describes your personal life while you are busy with your senior management responsibilities.

You now have teenage children who wish to conquer the world because they have seen their parents were able to do it best of the way. Ensuring they get right mentoring and direction from you or your mentor is a responsibility at this stage.

I have observed two points. Parents have built an empire but children want to pursue a normal life. They don't find a management role in the organization as colorful. They enjoy the freshness of joining a vibrant job.

Second point is more important to know, that your children stick with you because of what you are and not because what you have or what they can get out of you.

Development of leadership takes time and one should allow it to naturally grow by providing the necessary inputs in a timely manner.

ACTION EXERCISE

A Typical Day

- You are surrounded by people who respect you for what you are and not because of what you have.

- You are constantly in touch with your mentors and executive life coaches. It gives access to those knowledge which most of the senior leadership across the world practices at present.

- You have allocated specific time in your daily schedule to think deeply where you are heading to and what you are becoming, both in business and as human.

Learning Areas

- Read two books every week. Start with book summary of those books and then get into details. It can save time yet keep yourself updated.

- Strict regime on food and exercise. Aa a person of knowledge and wisdom, you need to care for your longevity, so that you can give back more.

- Any emotional outbursts causes more harm than the physical exertion and you know that well.

- Spending longer time with self can give lot of insights which can be implemented in business.

- You understand that he who gives more receives more.

- You have learnt to align with the order of nature, than forcing your individual interests.

Recommendations

- Leadership in organizations – Gary Yukl

- Discover your destiny – Robin Sharma

- 5 levels of leadership - John Maxwell

- The 80/20 rule – Robert Coach

- Art of living - Epictetus

- Life Strategies: Doing What Works, Doing What Matters – Phil McGraw

NAVEEN CHANDRA

MEET THE AUTHOR

Naveen Chandra comes with Information Technology background and has closely observed the changes, competitiveness, its effect on people, career and the general mindset towards professional and personal life.

Hailing from Mysore, Karnataka, India, is an alumnus of SJCE, Mysore and TAPMI, Bangalore. He has been actively involved in developing individuals and teams towards leadership through innovative trainings relevant to 21st century.

Mr. Chandra does so in a friendly, energized and hit to the point approach that inspires audience for lasting actions. Over the years, he has developed the ability to cut through the clutter which keeps most away from their heart's pursuit. His strategies are well defined, action oriented and reliable. He has worked successfully with individuals, teams, corporate leaders for better coherence and performance.

He strongly believes in making a difference to lives of others with the approach of *live by heart!*

www.naveenchandra.in

www.ingramcontent.com/pod-product-compliance
Lightning Source LLC
Chambersburg PA
CBHW031415210526
45464CB00005B/1889

www.ingramcontent.com/pod-product-compliance
Lightning Source LLC
Chambersburg PA
CBHW020642220526
45464CB00001B/266

The End